DICK KRECK

RICH PEOPLE BEHAVING BADLY

FULCRUM
GOLDEN, COLORADO

Cover photo: Socially prominent Denver clubman Courtland Dines cavorts with silent-screen stars Mabel Normand, center, and Edna Purviance on a jolly seagoing outing to Catalina Island off the coast of California. Courtesy of *The Denver Post*.

Library of Congress Cataloging-in-Publication Data
Names: Kreck, Dick, author.
Title: Rich people behaving badly / by Richard Kreck.
Description: Golden, CO : Fulcrum Publishing, [2016]
Identifiers: LCCN 2016006643 | ISBN 9781936218233 (paperback)
Subjects: LCSH: Scandals--Colorado--Case studies. | Crime--Colorado--Case studies. | Rich people--Colorado--Case studies. | Colorado--Social life and customs. | Colorado--History. | BISAC: HISTORY / United States / State & Local / West (AK, CA, CO, HI, ID, MT, NV, UT, WY). | TRUE CRIME / General.
Classification: LCC F776 .K74 2016 | DDC 978.8--dc23
LC record available at http://lccn.loc.gov/2016006643

Printed in the United States of America

0 9 8 7 6 5 4 3 2 1

Fulcrum Publishing
4690 Table Mountain Dr., Ste. 100
Golden, CO 80403
800-992-2908 • 303-277-1623
www.fulcrumbooks.com

ALSO BY DICK KRECK

Colorado's Scenic Railroads

Denver in Flames

Murder at the Brown Palace

Anton Woode: The Boy Murderer

Smaldone: The Untold Story of an American Crime Family

Hell on Wheels: Wicked Towns Along the Union Pacific Railroad

CONTENTS

ACKNOWLEDGMENTS

No history book gets written without support. Some of the people I need to thank:

First, my sharp-eyed editor, Alison Auch; the always-helpful staff at the Genealogy and Western History Department, Denver Public Library; Shaun Boyd, Local History Collection, Douglas County Library, Castle Rock, Colorado; Castle Rock Historical Society and Museum, Castle Rock, Colorado; Stacey Cline, Museum of Colorado Prisons, Cañon City, Colorado; Colorado State Archives; Coi Drummond-Gehrig, image sales/research, Genealogy and Western History Department, Denver Public Library; Vickie Makings, *The Denver Post* library; Faith Marcovecchio, my friend and sometime editor; Dianne Millican Miller; crack genealogist Loujean Rehn; Richard Schilling; Stephen H. Hart and Research Center at History Colorado; Lisa Studts, curator, Royal Gorge Regional Museum and History Center, Cañon City, Colorado; Ray Thal, Riverside Cemetery, Denver. And especially the scores of anonymous journalists who so vividly described too-human peccadilloes for our prying eyes.

AUTHOR'S NOTE

The public's interest in the naughty and sometimes murderous behavior of the rich and/or famous seems never-ending. It's the reason television "reality" shows and online gossip are wildly popular and why sensational trials and tribulations of stars and would-be stars capture our interest.

Historical research gives a broader perspective. The foibles of people, rich or poor, remain the same; only fashions change. Public respectability does not always translate into tidy private lives. One hundred years ago and down through the years, murders, infidelities, financial misdeeds, and just plain misbehavior have captured the media's attention. Literally, volumes have been written.

Included here are socialites such as Louise Sneed Hill, who created and ruled over Denver's "Sacred 36" circle of society and kept company with a dashing polo player; Jane Tomberlin, who met and fell in love with a "prince" in an elevator at the Brown Palace Hotel; Irene Nolan, who cavorted late into the night with her family priest; and prominent Denver clubman Courtland Dines, wounded during a frolic with two silent-screen stars in his Hollywood apartment.

And then there are the plain wrongdoers: Frederick Bonfils, co-founder of *The Denver Post*, dipping his fingers in the oily scandal of the Teapot Dome mess; Fred Ward, the car dealer who peddled Hudsons he didn't own; and Pastor Charles Blair, whose financial sleight of hand brought down his religious empire.

Two of the stories in this book are not about rich people, but nevertheless screamed for telling. Pearl O'Loughlin, married to a Denver cop and accused of killing her stepdaughter in 1930, deserved a closer look because it became clear to me that the evidence against her was questionable at best. She served twenty years of a life sentence and maintained her innocence until she was paroled in 1952. She may not have done it.

The story of early-day Denver prostitute Mattie Young is a cautionary episode that demonstrates the chaotic and often tragic life the brides of the multitudes led. The romanticized version in movies and on television of merry young women in flouncy dresses amid sumptuous surroundings doesn't begin to reflect the grinding day-to-day lives of desperation prostitutes led. Drugs, physical abuse, and suicides snuffed too many too young.

Portions of "The Butterfly," the tale of Isabel Springer, wife of a prominent Denver businessman; her two lovers; and the tragic shooting in 1911 appear in a longer version in my book *Murder at the Brown Palace*. It remains one of the city's most scandalous episodes.

And so it goes. They made us look.

CHAPTER 1

THE GREAT SCANDAL

WILLIAM NEWTON BYERS

A pistol-waving woman scorned is not to be trifled with.

On April 5, 1876, less than a week after a spring snowstorm buried Denver under a foot of snow, things heated up for William Newton Byers, a pioneer pillar of the community and owner/publisher of the *Rocky Mountain News*.

Robert Perkin in his book *The First Hundred Years*, the entertaining and informative history of the *News*, reasoned, "The scandal had nothing but the highest-quality ingredients. A pioneer and civic dignitary, strictly top of the heap, respected, envied by many, probably maliciously and privately disliked by some for his prominence and many honors. A beautiful young woman, a divorcee (practically scandalous in itself), and the rumors were that she was 'pretty fast.'"

Byers, who had hopes of becoming the soon-to-be state's first governor, found himself in the arms of a scandal that involved an ardent divorcée bent on his destruction, a series of passionate letters, an outraged wife, and a newspaper war.

Byers was a native of Ohio, and he spent the early 1850s as a surveyor in Iowa, on the West Coast, and in Omaha, Nebraska. He had a sudden revelation that it was time to move on to the wide-open spaces of Colorado and start a newspaper—a trade he knew nothing about. But he knew that a newspaper could be a driving force in the success of any new town.

He arrived in Denver at age twenty-eight on April 17, 1859, when the settlement at the confluence of the South Platte River and Cherry Creek was barely a year old. It was little more than a collection of shacks and teepees, with a population—liberally counted—of four hundred. Those who hit town were usually passing through on their way to the gold diggings in the Rockies. Within a year, more substantial structures were rising, and ten years after that, Denver became a rail hub and the major city in the Rocky Mountain region.

Byers had hauled an antiquated press and a few trays of type overland by wagon and he published the first issue of the *News* on April 23. It was his wife, Elizabeth—whom he married in Muscatine, Iowa, in 1854, and brought with him to Denver in '59—who suggested the paper's masthead. The paper immediately became a megaphone through which Byers, who saw a bright future where dirt and sagebrush reigned, bellowed the hopes and dreams of the fledgling village.

Byers, an upright and powerful citizen in his town, became involved in one of the more tawdry episodes in the city's history—what came to be known in the local prints as "The Great Scandal"—when he and Mrs. Hattie Sancomb became acquainted, and much more. She was a divorcée from Lawrence, Kansas, who possessed, observed one admirer, coal-gray eyes, auburn hair, and "a voice soft and her manner caressing." Unfortunately, no photograph of the apparently fetching Hattie is known to exist.

As a young milliner, Hattie was considering a move to Denver and wrote to Byers. He was then head of the Board of Immigration, and it was his mission to paint a rosy picture for all comers. As he did with all such inquiries, he encouraged her to relocate. After a brief stop in Denver to thank Byers, she continued on to Golden—then vying with Denver to become the region's leading town—where she reestablished her millinery business. It wasn't long before she began to suggest to Byers, now in his forties, that she would like to continue their relationship. Little wonder that she chose him from among her several admirers. He was handsome, with piercing eyes and a close-cropped beard in the style of Civil War hero Ulysses S. Grant. It was a leap year and Mrs. Sancomb took full advantage in her pursuit of Byers.

Byers conceded that what had been a business correspondence in the summer of 1871 became something more. In the latter part of 1872 they began a "closer acquaintance," he said. "During the winter of 1874–75 we met each other but three or four times, and nothing unusual took

William Newton Byers

Courtesy of the Western History and Genealogy Department, Denver Public Library, Z-2342

place until the spring of 1875 when Hattie took offense at some fancied neglect and began to write" after he tried to break off the relationship.

Did she write! She poison-penned a series of letters, perhaps as many as a hundred, in which she threatened Byers with mayhem: "You've made me hate you again with all the deadly hatred a woman can have for a man..."; "I will kill you. ... Wouldn't it be fun to put a few bullets, four, just four, through your heart"; and "All I ask is a glimpse of you, and my bullet will be well aimed. I will not miss." (See a sampling of her letters later in the chapter.)

She began to stalk him, on the street, at his home, and at the *News* offices. Byers recalled later, "Her second visit to my office was on Friday, March 31, the day of the recent heavy snowstorm, when she sat there all day, alternately threatening, crying, and coaxing the employees to get to me. She finally left in the evening but returned again on Saturday morning when the business manager was compelled to put her out as she again threatened to shoot, and drew her pistol." It was what famed journalist William Allen White found out as a young reporter in Eldorado, Kansas, when an angry young businesswoman took umbrage with something he had written and spent her days stalking him, "laying for me with 'patient and vigil long,' which controls a woman scorned." If Hattie's hate-filled letters threatened harm and death, Byers's correspondence promised only love and affection. In 1875, when their affair was in full bloom, he wrote to her with salutations that read, "My Dear, Darling Hattie" and "Darling Hattie," and concluded, "With warm kisses, ever truly yours."

In a story in the *News* on April 18, Byers claimed his letters were penned only "as nearly as possible to please her and keep her quiet." Their tone said otherwise. Even the pending showdown between Hattie and Byers didn't cool his ardor for her. In June 1876, three months after a dustup at the front door of his home, he wrote to her from Rollinsville, Colorado: "I received first word from my wife since I left home, and to the effect that she was so ill the second and third days after my departure that her recovery was despaired of. I am so glad that it is not my little Hattie."

In the same letter, he tried to reassure a suspicious Hattie that she was his only love interest. "I have not seen or heard from K. W. [*not otherwise identified*] since the note of which I wrote you, about the manuscript. I never have given her one particle of love. All my love belongs to Hattie." He closed with, "I want to be permitted to love you" and "God bless you, W."

The inevitable, and potentially fatal, showdown between the lovers unfolded in midday on April 5, 1876, practically on the doorstep of Byers's home at Colfax Avenue and Sherman Street, where the state office annex stands today.

In Byers's account, printed in the *Rocky Mountain Herald* only three days later, he took a horse-drawn streetcar from the *News* office near Fifteenth and Larimer Streets home for lunch, as he often did.

I took the streetcars at 12:20 o'clock, and occupied a seat near the entrance. When near opposite Courthouse Square, this woman made two or three attempts to get on the car while it was in motion but without success. The driver was apprised of her efforts and when he had partly stopped the car she stepped in and tumbled into my lap. I pushed her one side to a seat, without attracting much attention from the other three or four passengers.

In the meantime, she repeatedly asked me to get out and walk with her, as she had something she wanted to talk over. I refused her request, and told her that if she wished to settle this matter she could see me at my house, and that I would walk with her there. When the car was about two blocks from my residence, I got out and she did the same. She again requested me to walk with her. When some three hundred feet from the railroad track, and near the corner of a vacant lot, she halted and demanded to know what I proposed to do with her proposition, meaning the one she made about the time of my visit to Golden. I refused to talk on the subject and started towards home, when she drew her pistol and attempted to shoot.

I held both her arms firmly for a time, until my wife, seeing the struggle from a window of the house, jumped into her buggy— which was standing near the door—and drove rapidly to where we were. I let go her hands and jumped into the buggy, when she fired a shot that passed behind the seat and lodged near the residence of E. W. Keyes, whose little boy narrowly escaped being hurt.

In the excitement the driving lines got caught in the single-tree so that the horse made a complete circle where this woman was standing, pistol in hand. When within a few feet of me she attempted to fire the second time but the pistol did not go off. We drove to the house and she followed, but my son, taking in the situation, stopped her at the gate. She put her pistol in his face but as he happened to have a revolver with him she concluded not to shoot.

Elizabeth Byers

Courtesy of the Western History and Genealogy Department, Denver Public Library, Z-2336

*I drove the horse to the stable and my wife went through the
house and opened the front door, where [Elizabeth's] pistol got tangled in the sleeve of her dress and went off merely by accident. This
is the only shot that was fired at the house. A messenger was sent
on horseback to call an officer, and she, noticing him depart, walked
away from the gate, and had gone two or three blocks before Officer
Sanders arrested her.*

No one was injured by the gunplay.

Hattie Sancomb's version, retold in the April 15 *Golden Weekly Globe*,
charted a different course. She, the story said, clai med that the two of
them were "sauntering along the street in confidential conversation in
the direction of Mr. Byers's house, he having his arm within hers, when
Mrs. Byers, seeing them, drove up in a carriage and, calling upon Mr. B
to get into the carriage, threatened him with injury if he did not obey."
Hattie claimed it was Mrs. Byers who fired the shot that narrowly missed
the neighbor boy. In her version, they were all packing guns. Mrs. Byers,
according to Hattie, said at the house, "Throw down your pistol and you
may come in." She declined and the police soon arrived to take her to jail.

Byers's fellow publishers and editors remained silent on the confrontation until his friend and former employee George West let it all
out, printing some of the letters in his *Golden Transcript*. It was open season on William and Hattie. Their letters began turning up in the *Transcript* and its rival *Golden Globe*. It wasn't until April 16 that the *News* felt
compelled to jump into the fray with a stirring defense of its editor. In
an editorial probably dictated and certainly approved by Byers, the *News*
said, "It had become necessary to make the matter public in order to
clear up the 'distorted and false' statements of the *Golden Transcript*. Mrs.
Sancomb, divorced in Lawrence on a charge of adultery with one Colonel
Burns, had for nearly a year past kept up a series of attacks and a round of
persecution upon Mr. Byers."

Never completely cordial, things between the area's newspapers
grew more heated. Papers in Golden hinted that Hattie was not Byers's
first dalliance outside his marriage. *The News's* editors countered with
dark hints that West was "closely intimate" with Mrs. Sancomb.

The city's other newspapers tried to keep their distance but defend-
ed Byers and his tarnished image. *The Herald*, owned and edited by Owen

Goldrick, a former employee at the *News* and founder of Denver's first school, suggested it was nothing but a scheme to squeeze money from Byers: "We consider that Mr. Byers was a big fool to allow himself to become attached, intrigued or inveigled into any such enlarging alliances with any such divorced woman, who he knew that she knew he wasn't a single man, but was, on the contrary, 'just the oyster' for baiting and beating into blackmail or blacker misfortune."

Mrs. Sancomb's behavior and the whole incident went before a grand jury, but Byers's lawyers, wary of dragging out the scandal any longer, withdrew their complaint.

The historical record on Hattie after the court case is scanty. In March, only two weeks before the shooting, a brief item in the *Golden Weekly Globe* reported that "Mrs. Sancomb is disposing of her stock of millinery and fancy goods and will remove to Denver," but the following December a small advertisement appeared in the paper for her shop on Washington Avenue in Golden.

Byers survived the shooting and scandal but it destroyed his hopes of becoming governor. He had to stand aside when John L. Routt was elected the new state's first governor on October 3, 1876. He sold the *News* in 1878 and became Denver's postmaster in March 1879. Later he became vice president of the Denver Tramway Company, and tried and failed to make the mountain town of Hot Sulphur Springs a resort for well-to-do tourists.

The blackest mark on his career of boosting and building took place in 1864, when Byers and his close friend Governor John Evans precipitated one of the darkest chapters in Colorado. As governor of Colorado Territory, Evans was in charge of Indian affairs, a task for which he was woefully unprepared. With the help of Byers and his *Rocky Mountain News*, Evans whipped Denver citizens into a frenzy, warning that bands of Cheyenne and Arapaho were planning an attack on Denver.

All the war talk led to the establishment of the Third Colorado Regiment, led by Colonel John Chivington, and his troops swept down on a Cheyenne and Arapaho village on November 29, 1864, killing as many as two hundred Indians, mostly women, children, and old men.

Byers's role in the tragedy at Sand Creek is overshadowed by his legacy as a builder of the region he loved. There are streets and schools named for him in Denver, and a mountain peak near Fraser, which he summited when he was seventy years old, bears his name.

He was part of a small coterie of business leaders and friends—one that would come to include David Moffat, John Evans, and Robert Speer—that ruled the political and economic life of the city well into the twentieth century. The tramway company, the water department, and the city hall were their fiefdom. Jerome Smiley, whose *History of Denver* is the quintessential work on the city's early days, said of the energetic Byers, "The life history of Mr. Byers since he became a citizen of Denver at that time forms a large part of the history of the city."

It was Byers and his friends and associates who brought the telegraph and the first railroad to Denver. He was a tireless champion of statehood for Colorado and helped found the University of Denver, the Colorado Historical Society, the Natural History Society, and the city's first library. In a retrospective of Byers's life in the *News* in 1999, historian David F. Halaas raved, "It was almost as though Denver was his personal creation. He was out to promote Denver, to help make it a permanent thing."

Byers died in Denver on March 25, 1903, one month after his seventy-second birthday, and is buried at Fairmount Cemetery.

Hattie Sancomb, the scorned lover, did not take the breakup gracefully. Beginning in 1875, she wrote a series of scathing and threatening letters to William Byers and to his wife, Elizabeth. Here are excerpts of some of them:

June 1, 1875
I'll not fawn on you till you kick me. That is the mettle you are made of, but you shall not kick me; but, by all that is black, bad, and terrible, I'll do some kicking one day.

౸౷

June 3, 1875

I have dedicated the rest of my life to your misery, and be assured, though I cease to speak of this, I shall hang about you like an incubus, and blasted shall you be. I simply warn you that you have a desperate enemy upon your track. You are only dear to me as an object of revenge.

Oh, infernal villain, if I had you here I'd plant my fingers in your eyes and tear them from their sockets.

Oh, how I hate you. You shall not long exist. I'll blot out your existence before you shall ever know who dealt the blow to you.

෨ඁ

July 3, 1875

Great God, I have now nothing but the most blasphemous curses for you. You can do nothing now to save you or your family.

Ah, my friend, such letters as the one this morning will not do for me. A letter without kisses quiets me in a measure. Without them all is lost to me but my thirst for revenge; the blackest, damning revenge which I will have so help me God.

෨ඁ

Golden, Sept. 1875

Receiving no word from you, I have thought it best to inform you I would be down to see [you] to-morrow. You were too cowardly to write me, so as not to give me a reply in time to go down. Now look here. You've made me hate you again with all the deadly hatred a woman can have for a man, and you have always lied like hell to me, expecting to "put me off," and that won't answer.

You have driven me crazy again with only the desire in my heart to take your life, and bring destruction to your family. I'll do it, or hope God my strike me dead if I don't. Damn again and G-d damn you. I will kill you. ... Wouldn't it be fun to put a few bullets, four, just four, through your heart. When and where I can have the pleasure of killing you cold and lifeless in your regalia. For pleasure it will be to me. G-d damn you, damn you, damn you.

❧

Jan. 8, 1876

I demand that you come to see me next Sunday. Don't write me that you won't as I command you to come to me next Sunday—and that I love you and that I care to see you, but only to punish you for your damning lies to me for so long.

I shall let you live to endure that punishment and then I repeat to you: I mean murder, damn you and G-d damn you. I mean MURDER; do you understand? I mean MURDER.

CHAPTER 2

THE WICKEDEST STREET

MATTIE YOUNG

A woman whose moniker was "Calamity Jane" was no doubt trouble.

But she wasn't *that* Calamity Jane. No, Mattie Young was not the famous frontier heroine of the West; however she did have her own adventurous life. Mattie left her Iowa home at a young age; had a baby girl when she was sixteen; and in early 1878, at the age of twenty-four, she wound up in Denver as a working girl in the city's infamous red-light district on Holladay Street.

Holladay (later renamed Market) was the epicenter of the city's district, one where more than a thousand prostitutes worked in high-end parlor houses for $5 a trick, or in the shabbier "cribs," where love could be rented for anywhere from 10 to 25 cents. One patron of the cribs, whose girls were interested in turning as much profit as they could as quickly as they could, complained that a typical encounter lasted less than five minutes, and he kept his pants on.

The occupants of brothels, some from respectable families, worked under colorful sobriquets—"Ella the Wolf," "Few Clothes Molly," "Nellie the Pig," and "Wide-Ass Nellie," among them.

The year 1878–79 was one of incredible growth for Denver. The discovery of silver in Leadville, high in the Rockies, brought about a flood of "newcomers [who] found employment before they could find lodgings," wrote historian Jerome Smiley. Rents soared, building boomed, and tourism flourished. Where there were men, prostitutes followed.

Denver's red-light district was a muddy street lined with shabby buildings, an uninviting place to call home for Mattie Young and her sister prostitutes. Here, a bride of the multitudes stands on the lookout for customers at 2130 Market Street.

Courtesy of the Western History and Genealogy Department, Denver Public Library, Z-8931

Saloons and brothels were an integral part of early western towns, because they attracted young men and their money. However, until the early 1860s, Denver's saloons, dance halls, and gambling parlors—all of which were good points of contact for girls who liked to have fun—were primitive affairs, often little more than tents thrown up over dirt floors, where cheap whiskey and the pleasures of gambling and women were readily available. Lizzie Preston is credited with opening the first true parlor house in 1862 or 1863, launching Holladay's tawdry reputation. The city's more upstanding residents were accepting of the activity on Holladay, as long as the working girls stayed in their neighborhood.

One local newspaper writer branded Holladay "the most wicked street in the west." Cy Martin wrote in *The Denver Republican*:

> *Approximately one thousand "brides of the multitude" were avail-*
> *able in the imposing parlor houses or lowly cribs which lined both*
> *sides of the street for three blocks. The cribs were just wide enough*
> *for a door and two narrow windows. Each crib contained two tiny*
> *rooms—a parlor in front, a boudoir in back. "Come on in, dearie,"*
> *was the customary invitation, but if the prospect did not respond,*
> *the girl might grab his hat and pitch it inside her room. Some of the*
> *cribs displayed signs which shocked even the hardened residents of*
> *pioneer Denver.*

Mattie Young might have labored in anonymity with her sisters in love-for-sale, except for a spectacular and reckless carriage dash through the streets that ended with her death one hot summer evening in August 1878.

It was a year of extreme weather; there was even a solar eclipse. A very cold winter was followed by a blistering summer, during which the high temperatures in August averaged 88 degrees, topped 100 degrees three times, and reached 105 on August 8—a record that still stands. August 21, a sunny Wednesday afternoon, was a perfect setting for a jolly romp through the heart of the city's nascent business district in today's LoDo.

Mattie and Nellie Smith, another denizen of her parlor house, decided to take a joyride with two young rakes, Morgan Collins and a man known only as "George." Newspaper accounts of the day reported that their "dates" were drunk when they set out. Unless it was the girls' day off, they broke one of the cardinal rules of the houses of ill fame—getting drunk on the job. "A drunk," warned one madam, "is no good as a whore. You can't hide her breath, and she doesn't do her work in style."

The two young women could be forgiven if they decided to take off on a lark. A harlot's lot was not an easy one. "Fighting, drunkenness, and mayhem filled the air of the brothel," wrote Anne M. Butler in *Daughters of Joy, Sisters of Misery*, her study of prostitutes in the Old West. "Even the most ordinary customer might unexpectedly turn on a prostitute; or some hapless inmate could get caught in the crossfire of feuding customers." Life on the row was one of "sordidness and corruption." Trapped in such an existence, prostitutes often chose suicide as a way out. Laudanum, a potent mix of alcohol and opium, was most popular, but others dispatched themselves with overdoses of morphine, chloroform, or by ingesting out-and-out poisons such as strychnine, which led to a particularly gruesome death.

Josie Washburn, a former madam in Omaha, Nebraska, gave a chilling insight into life behind the daintily curtained windows in her memoir, *The Underworld Sewer*:

> *Crowd after crowd come to the different doors and yell for admission. They are drunk, we fear them; WE NEVER GET OVER THIS FEAR, although we have seen the same performances daily year after year. A drunken bunch has arrived, they are young and handsome fellows, they use vile language. They are society dudes and imagining they are making a hit with our girls by exhibiting their toughness, failing to find an appreciative audience they pinch and hurt the girls just to hear them scream, and curse them and call them names.*

It was far from the glamorous, fun-filled life too often portrayed in movies and on television. The girls, whose prime earning years were between fifteen and thirty years old, rarely lasted more than four years in the trade. It was not financially rewarding, and putting aside money to escape the life was next to impossible because they often were supporting a husband or boyfriend, their families, or, in rare cases, their own children. Except in the very high-end brothels, the clientele consisted of a transient population of miners, laborers, cowboys, bullwhackers, soldiers, and drifters, none of them financially well off themselves. One way prostitutes could enhance their income was to rob their clients of money, watches, and jewelry if they were too amorous or too drunk to notice. Victims could complain to the police, but they had little interest in pursuing such cases.

A "boarder" might split her night's earnings fifty-fifty with the madam, but out of her half she had to pay for her room and board and for clothing. In addition, she was always under the threat of contracting venereal disease, arrest (even though crooked cops were frequently paid off by the house), and violence from patrons or other prostitutes.

On the afternoon of August 21, 1878, Mattie and Nellie took a break from their day-to-day toil with the adventurous Mattie on the reins of a rented double carriage. But after a stop for supper and drinks at the Potter House on 370 Blake Street, Collins, a young man from Deer Trail far out on the plains east of Denver, took over, with Mattie riding on his lap.

The high-spirited foursome careened down Blake Street at a fast trot, sped across Fifteenth Street, and barreled through a crowd gathered to watch firefighters extinguish a blaze. One spectator was struck and knocked to the ground, bruised but alive. Near the Lindell Hotel at Eleventh and Larimer Streets on the south side of Cherry Creek, the reckless foursome struck another man, John F. Smith, who suffered three broken ribs.

And then it was off to Denver Park, also known as Denver Gardens and, later, Olympic Gardens. The park was on the north side of the South Platte River, about where West Colfax Avenue crosses the river today. Set amidst a large shaded grove of cottonwood trees, the park was a favorite hangout for the city's younger set, where they could drink and raise hell beyond the prying eyes of Denver authorities.

The area was noteworthy for two previous dustups. In 1860, twenty-two-year-old William Duffield, a soldier in the First Colorado Cavalry, and a small group of drunken pals wandered over to Aunt Betsy's, a brothel on the Platte across the river from Cherry Creek and adjacent to the park. The rowdy bunch demanded entrance by kicking the front door, and then hurled stones through the establishment's windows. The response was gunfire from within. Young Duffield fell, crying out, "Don't run, boys, I am shot!" They ran. Duffield, struck in the shoulder, died at the scene.

Seventeen years later, on August 24, 1877, two of the city's more prominent members of the local demimonde squared off in Denver Park during a night of rampant hilarity. Mattie Silks and Katie Fulton, rivals in the sex trade and both with avid interests in Mattie's "boyfriend," Cort Thomson, fell into an argument over him. Cort got between them and slugged Katie, knocking her to the ground. For good measure, he kicked her while she was down, breaking her nose. Others got involved and the fight was broken up, but later that evening someone took a shot at Cort, wounding him slightly as he drove his carriage through downtown.

Opened in 1876, the park was owned by the Denver Brewing Company and, naturally, featured beer among its many amenities, which included a picnic pavilion, a freak museum, a mineral exhibit, and a small zoo of native animals. There was also a bar that featured wine, liquor, and plenty of beer. It was, said management, all aboveboard. A sign greeted the high-flying foursome of Mattie and her friends at the entrance to the park's pedestrian walks and carriage paths, warning, "NO IMPROPER CHARACTERS ADMITTED!"

More drinks followed, with Mattie and Nellie joining in. "Mattie got the drunkest," Nellie testified later. When it came time to leave, Collins attempted to swing the carriage around but it capsized into a ditch. Three of the riders escaped unhurt, but Mattie, thrown under the carriage, suffered serious internal injuries, undiagnosed at the time.

Famed Denver lawman Sam Howe later told a coroner's hearing that he pursued the carriage to Denver Park, but that by the time he arrived, three of the partiers had disappeared. He took Mattie to the city jail, where she spent the night before being taken to the county hospital.

At 11 p.m. four days later, Mattie was dead. A coroner's inquest concluded that she died "from internal injuries which involved the kidneys together with congestion of the womb and bladder." Her health already was poor because she had suffered a miscarriage only a month before. The jury said "that [the] deceased came to her death from the result of injuries received by the upsetting of a carriage near Denver Park, caused by reckless driving." Collins later turned himself in and was fined $50 for assault on the two injured men and tried for cruelty to animals. He went unpunished for Mattie's death.

Prostitution may have been tolerated, but impairing the safety of citizens was not. The newspapers scolded such goings-on. Then as now, young people were fond of speed. *The Denver Times* editorialized: "If they choose to imperil their own lives, the public might look on with commendable complacency. But innocent parties ... must not be placed in peril of life and limb for the privilege of giving hoodlums the opportunity of holding their drunken orgies."

The Rocky Mountain News echoed that sentiment, sending a warning to all horse-powered speed demons: "The death of Mattie Young—other than the moral it too forcibly points—teaches a practical and timely lesson of the dangers of fast driving, which seems to be tolerated in Denver to a greater extent than anywhere in the country, and one which the end of the unfortunate girl should bring home with great force in the minds of our municipal authorities."

Mattie's funeral on August 26 attracted a large crowd of "female associates," who bought her a casket, a rich burial robe, an elaborate floral cross to sit atop the coffin, and a burial plot. Her remains were conveyed to Riverside Cemetery at the northern edge of the city, but there is no marker on her grave, either because her friends couldn't afford one or because those interred near her preferred that she remain anonymous. "Let charity and forgetfulness cover the sins of the unfortunate woman," intoned *The Times*.

CHAPTER 3

THE BUTTERFLY

ISABEL PATTERSON SPRINGER

"One by one the petals fell from the blooms of the primrose path, to bring her at last into the tangle of thorns which snarled themselves at the end, which enmeshed her, tore at her with their poison-tipped lances, which dragged her downward, downward to the mire."

Courtney Ryley Cooper's flowery obituary for Isabel Patterson Springer on the front page of *The Denver Post* on April 20, 1917, wrote an unglamorous finish to a decidedly glamorous woman.

All her life, Isabel had drawn men to her, but she made abysmal choices in those she chose to share her life with.

When she was only twenty years old and living in St. Louis, she married John E. Folck, a traveling shoe salesman—a marriage unhappy almost from the first day they wed in 1900. He drank heavily and frequently, pounded on her with his fists, and showered her with abusive language. The marriage fell apart in 1906, and Isabel went back to her gay lifestyle among the young social set, where she became known as "The Butterfly."

Among her "fast" set was a young adventurer named Tony von Phul (pronounced "von Fool"). He was a connoisseur of beautiful (and, often, married) women, a dedicated balloonist, a former ranch hand, a racecar driver, and something of a rough-around-the-edges bully who lugged around a gun (or two). He was smitten with her.

Shortly after her separation from her abusive husband, Isabel—an exceptional beauty with dark eyes set in a cherubic face and blessed with an ample bosom—met Denver businessman and civic leader John W. Springer, passing through St. Louis on a horse-buying trip to Kentucky.

Isabel Patterson Springer
Author's collection

She immediately saw that the well-respected—and wealthy—Springer was a far better catch than the volatile von Phul.

In the summer of 1906, before her divorce was final, Isabel traveled with Springer to Denver, where he loved to show her off around town in his cherry-red coach pulled by a four-horse team of gleaming black Percherons. Her arrival created a stir among the city's social set. "We always thought John W. was pretty fair looking," crooned a *Post* columnist, "but his wife is a stunning beauty, and it is safe to prophesy that the Springer home is going to be a social center." "As queenly as a three-sheet poster of Lillian Russell," said another.

Springer was forty-seven and she was twenty-seven when they married at the Jefferson Hotel in St. Louis on April 27, 1907. The Springers' social life, centered on their rooms at the Brown Palace Hotel, was indeed a focal point for society, but their parties focused on Springer's political career. A two-story mansion at 930 Washington Street in the city's tony Quality Hill neighborhood, and 12,000-acre cattle and horse ranch, complete with a stone mansion, in what is today's Highlands Ranch suburb, augmented the suite at the Brown.

Isabel was clearly a trophy wife for the much older Springer, whose first wife died of tuberculosis in 1904. He parked his new bride at the Brown to revel in the comforts of the hotel and went on with his busy life in ranching, politics, and considerable civic activities, marked by frequent business trips to the East. He appeared to be unaware of Isabel's extramarital activities.

Isabel was charming and flirtatious with the opposite sex; she liked it when men complimented her on her beauty. Though she was carefree and unconventional in her personal life, she was far from emancipated; John Springer took care of her worldly needs. She lived at the elegant Brown Palace Hotel with maids, housekeepers, and chauffeurs to wait on her.

A young and adventurous woman like Isabel was not content with reading magazines, attending tea parties, and taking trips to the theater. Her restlessness soon fastened on Frank Henwood, a young rambler who blew into Denver late in 1910 and immediately became part of local society, partly because he had grown up in well-to-do circumstances and enjoyed the high life, and partly because he was desperate to forge a new career for himself and needed moneyed contacts to finance his new enterprise as a promoter for a gas company. Springer was Henwood's perfect target. It wasn't long after their first meeting in Springer's office

John W. Springer
Author's collection

that Isabel was calling Henwood "Frank," and she became "Sassy" to the dashing gas salesman. Such immediate familiarity was almost unheard of in that era.

Soon, she and Frank were sharing weekend visits to the baronial country mansion, sometimes with her husband, sometimes just the two of them. Meanwhile, Isabel had not entirely left behind her St. Louis beau, Tony von Phul. Early in 1911, she took to writing him letters bursting with passion—"I can hardly bear to be away from you I miss you so much" and "Just a little note tonight to let you know your little sweetheart is thinking of you." She even begged him to come to Denver to visit her, despite her new diversion.

When von Phul got wind of Henwood's attentions to Isabel, he threatened to show her letters to her husband unless she spurned the in-terloping Frank and resumed her relationship with him. Isabel turned to Frank, asking him to retrieve the incriminating love letters. He, of course, was happy to oblige, but only if she would pen a note to von Phul, telling him that things were over between them.

The triangle began to come undone in late May 1911. In a bizarre twist, all the principals were residing at the Brown. Henwood and von Phul first encountered each other in the lobby of the hotel, not by chance. When von Phul checked in, the clerk handed him a note from Isabel, that without a doubt Henwood had dictated to her. It read, in part, "This is just to let you know that someone knows a great deal. Therefore, under no circumstances, telephone me or try to communicate with me in any way."

Not surprisingly, von Phul was furious. He stormed out of the hotel and headed down Seventeenth Street to the stately Daniels & Fisher department store to meet with Isabel and her mother, who traveled with her frequently. Right behind him was the ardent Henwood, and the two men confronted each other in the palm-bedecked shoe department.

There were harsh, sometimes vulgar words, and the two agreed to go back to von Phul's room at the hotel and talk things out. They shared a cab, neither man willing to leave his rival behind. Once in von Phul's fifth-floor room, the confrontation became physical after Henwood de-manded the return of Isabel's letters. The much beefier von Phul knocked Henwood to the floor and threatened to shoot him, "but they would have it on me." Henwood happily retreated to his room on the seventh floor.

Frantic, Isabel was trying to juggle the emotions of two admirers, neither of whom was about to back down. The fleeting hours of May 23 were filled with meetings in her rooms, in hallways, in Henwood's room, in public places.

On the evening of May 24, the Springers, Henwood, and von Phul went, not together, to the Broadway Theater, which was walking distance from the Brown, to see a performance of "Follies of 1910." After the show, about 11:30 p.m., the Springers retired to their sixth-floor suite, and Henwood and von Phul, each probably knowing what he would find, adjourned to the Marble Bar in the Brown Palace.

Like pieces in a deadly game of chess, the players rearranged themselves along the bar. Von Phul, still steaming from two days of nasty encounters with Henwood, commented to his companion, "There's that son of a bitch I licked, and I ought to lick him again." Soon enough, the two men were standing next to each other.

Henwood, still full of hope that he could get Isabel's letters, was apologetic. "Won't you reconsider what happened yesterday afternoon?"

Von Phul wanted none of it. "I'm going upstairs and I am going to grab that gray-haired son of a bitch by the hair and pull him out of there and show him who is master here."

Henwood responded, heatedly, "You can't get that over on me."

Eyes fixed on Henwood, von Phul snarled, "I will get you first." Von Phul followed his remark with a quick and unexpected backhand to Henwood's jaw, sending him sprawling to the barroom floor. Unfortunately for von Phul, Henwood, afraid the bigger man would carry out his threats, had gone out that day and bought a five-shot .38. Someone in the crowded barroom shouted, "He's going to shoot!" Henwood emptied the gun, hitting von Phul three times. Worse luck for Henwood, the fusillade also struck and fatally wounded George Copeland, innocently enjoying a post-theater cocktail before catching a train home. It was for Copeland's death that Henwood would go on trial twice.

Von Phul, struck in the wrist, shoulder, and stomach, staggered to a nearby lounge and collapsed in a large leather chair, surrounded by bystanders, whom he reassured, "I'm all right, boys. I don't think I'm seriously injured, and I wish some of you would wire my father in St. Louis that I'm all right and not to pay attention to the newspaper reports he reads."

Twelve hours later, he was dead.

Henwood waited patiently for the police in the hotel lobby after the shooting and was unapologetic. He was sure the town would praise him

Frank Henwood
Author's collection

Tony von Phul
Author's collection

for getting rid of a home wrecker like von Phul. The newspapers, however, expressed shock at the prevalent habit of mixing alcohol and firearms. Still, women showered him with gifts in his small city jail cell.

After highly publicized trials in 1911 and 1913, he was ruled guilty of second-degree murder and given life in the first trial, and in the second he was ruled guilty of first-degree murder and sentenced to death. During his first trial, a rapt courtroom listened as the Springers' housekeeper related how, on one of Isabel and Frank's visit to the ranch, Isabel fell from her horse and twisted her ankle. Frank gallantly carried her to her second-floor bedroom—and didn't come out for two days. The housekeeper said the maid made several trips to Isabel's bedroom at the ranch to deliver trays of whiskey. The next morning, she said, she found Mrs. Springer's nightgown "torn into strips in front and about the neck." Asked what condition Mrs. Springer's bed was in, she replied, "It was rumpled and in great disorder."

After his second conviction, Henwood was shipped off to the state penitentiary in Cañon City, Colorado. A life filled with fits of temper and ill behavior became even more unbalanced with a death sentence hanging over him. Even though the governor commuted his sentence to life, Frank took to hiding under his bed on Fridays, which were the traditional hanging days at the prison.

Henwood was released from Cañon City in 1922 and moved to New Mexico, where he was determined to make a fresh start. He changed his name, found a job in a hotel, and was doing well until he pulled a gun on a woman who refused to marry him. That earned him a return to prison, where he lived out his life until September 28, 1929.

Though he never accepted responsibility for what he had done to the Springers' marriage and for the fact that he had taken two men's lives, Henwood conceded near the end of his life, "I have regrets."

Only days after Sassy's other attractions were splashed across Denver's newspapers, Springer divorced Isabel for "wholly disregarding her marital vows" and continued his business and political aspirations. He had one grand moment left: with his usual oratorical flourishes, he delivered the eulogy at William "Buffalo Bill" Cody's elaborate funeral in 1917. He remarried in 1915, to another much-younger woman, and lived out his life in the southern suburb of Littleton, where he died on January 10, 1945.

After her divorce, Isabel slipped out of town for Chicago and then to New York City, where she tried to resume her career as a model and sometime actress in silent films, but alcohol and drugs soon robbed her of her vivacious beauty. She died almost penniless in a charity hospital on March 28, 1917. She was thirty-seven years old.

Those who had praised her poise and beauty when she arrived in Denver as Springer's eye-catching wife turned on her. Alice Rohe, society columnist for the *Rocky Mountain News,* intoned, "It is when a woman begins to enthrall men without intellect but through sheer physical lures and sex attractions that she descends from the class of great courtesans into the mire of unnamable creatures."

Writing in *The Post,* well-known "sob sister" Frances "Pinky" Wayne branded Isabel "a seducer, not unlike many young women who manipulate men. The easiest way they have found is to assume the 'eternal feminine' pose."

The woman who dazzled Denver society and drew men to her with her beauty and flirtatious ways became a footnote in the history of the hotel and the city.

CHAPTER 4

THE FLOWER-FACED VAMPIRE

GERTRUDE GIBSON PATTERSON

Her fragile beauty masked a dark secret: She shot her invalid husband to death. In the back. In self-defense.

The year 1911 was littered with groundbreaking events—Roald Amundsen reached the South Pole, *Titanic* was launched, and ground was broken for Fenway Park in Boston.

But no event was whispered about more than when Gertrude Gibson Patterson went on trial for murder in Denver on November 20, 1911. It had all the earmarks of a delicious window into morals of the upper class: Did her husband sell her to a much older man for $1,500? Did she lure her husband to his death? Whom did the murder weapon belong to?

Before her trial began, the city's four daily newspapers had extraordinary access to Gertrude in her cell in the county jail. Lengthy interviews appeared almost daily. Reporters gushed over her. "Mrs. Patterson is an appealing type in her girlishness and fresh young beauty," Mildred Geddes fluttered in *The Denver Times*. "Her hair is golden brown and her large brown eyes have the softness and innocence of a child's." *The Denver Republican* described her in goddess-like terms: "She has large,

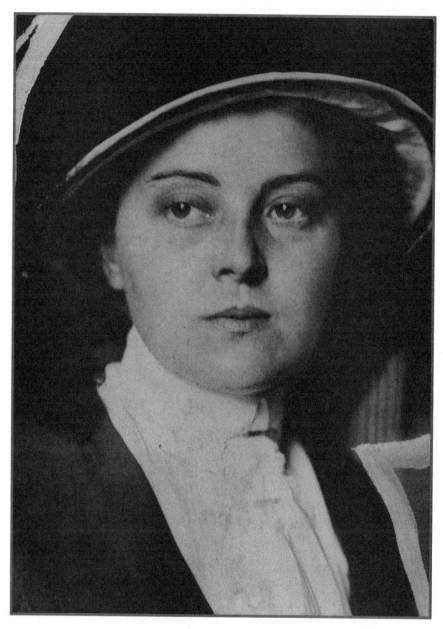

Gertrude Gibson Patterson was only sixteen years old
when she traveled to Europe with Chicago financier Emil Strouss.
Did her husband, Charles "Chick" Patterson, sell her for
$1,500? She shot Chick in the back near Richthofen Castle on
September 25, 1911, then claimed he committed suicide.

Rocky Mountain News, courtesy of the Western History and Genealogy Department, Denver Public Library

lustrous brown eyes, her nose is almost perfectly formed, and her mouth is one of those small bow-shaped, spoiled mouths that the poets declare were made for kisses. Hers is a doll-like beauty." Thirty-five years after the trial, noted Denver newspaperman Lee Casey was moved to reminisce that Gertrude "had the nicest legs that were ever planted in a defendant's booth."

On her first courtroom appearance, a bystander commented, "Standing there, her large brown eyes glowing in a face of childlike loveliness, her tiny hands clasped above her breast, her charming figure clothed in a blue tailleur suit, her sunny brown hair crowned by a blue-plumed turban, was the self-widowed defendant. Her lips, parted over pearly teeth, uttered a voiceless appeal." She was, said another, "dainty as a Dresden figurine."

Gertrude Gibson was born in St. Louis to a family of ten children and grew up in the small mining community of Sandoval, Illinois. It didn't hold much fascination for her. At thirteen, she was suspended from school for "improper conduct" after she and one of her sisters ran off with two men, one of them a saloonkeeper, to nearby Breese, Illinois. Her father enlisted the local marshal to fetch them.

When she was sixteen, she took a trip with her sister to Chicago, where she met millionaire clothing manufacturer Emil W. Strouss. He was smitten immediately. She was young, barely educated, and full of country ways. Strouss, a bachelor thirty-five years her senior, decided to make Gertrude his project in the manner of Eliza Doolittle in *Pygmalion*. He gave her music lessons, outfitted her in the latest fashions, and even bought her an electric automobile. Writing in her unpublished memoir, Gertrude recalled, "We grew to be great friends. He was much older than I. At the time I met him my hair was down my back in a braid."

To further her education and with her parents' permission, Strouss took Gertrude to Paris—"His intentions always seemed honorable"—where she learned fluent French, studied the arts that let her move easily through the upper classes, and mingled with business and political leaders.

When they returned to Chicago, it wasn't long before they were living together as husband and wife in the exclusive Stratford Hotel, although they weren't legally married and never would be.

She wanted for nothing, except Strouss kept putting off their marriage, making her "miserable and unhappy." She began to look for other opportunities and met handsome young athlete Charles "Chick" Patterson—a sandy-haired, blue-eyed former high school football player—at a skating rink, and spilled to him everything about her life and disappointment with the millionaire. Their relationship ripened until she encouraged him to travel to California with her, where they were married at Carmel-by-the-Sea on October 1, 1908. Despite the marriage, she took a second trip to Europe with Strouss to act, she said, as his interpreter at a business conference. Patterson let her go after she gave him $1,500 she got from Strouss.

Her marriage to Patterson was a contentious relationship almost from the beginning; her complaints included that he never worked during their three-year marriage. He spent his time, she said, drinking at night and sleeping half the day. "He was a drunkard." Living in Chicago and strapped for cash, she opened a boarding house but couldn't keep up with Charles's spendthrift and nonproductive ways. Finally, she went to Strouss and asked for help. He gave her $1,500. She said it was a wedding gift from him. Patterson said it was the price of letting his wife travel to Europe with Strouss.

Charles was stricken with pneumonia in February 1910. When it ripened into tuberculosis in October, the couple moved to Denver for his health. He was among a tidal wave of what became known as "lungers," sufferers of consumption who flocked to the Mile High City for its clean air and dry climate, hoping it would produce a cure. The couple also hoped to patch up their rocky marriage with a move out of Chicago. He was admitted to the Agnes Memorial Sanatorium in what is now the Lowry neighborhood, where she visited him often. At first, they rented a small house at 1463 South Clarkson Street and then, to be closer to the sanitarium, she bought a bungalow at what the local newspapers said was 1008 Steele Street, although there was no such street number then, and there isn't one now.

Patterson periodically prevailed on Gertrude to extract more and more money from Strouss. When none was forthcoming, he threatened to file an alienation of affection lawsuit for $25,000 against the millionaire. In September 1911, Gertrude filed for divorce from Charles.

On the morning of September 25, 1911, Gertrude and Charles met, presumably to discuss the pending divorce, at the corner of East Eighth Avenue and Olive Street. They walked five blocks through the Montclair neighborhood, even though he had shrunk to 115 pounds and his lungs were so badly deteriorated from TB that any sort of physical activity was exhausting. They eventually arrived outside the stone-and-iron wall in front of the Richthofen Castle, a thirty-five-room mansion built in 1887 at 7020 East Twelfth Avenue by Baron Walter von Richthofen, uncle of the famed German World War I flying ace.

The discussion between Gertrude and Charles quickly turned heated. She confronted him with a newspaper clipping that described his lawsuit. A sandstone bust of German emperor Frederick Barbarossa glowered down on the proceedings from one corner of the castle.

A shouting match ensued. It was reported that Gertrude came armed with a revolver in her purse. She told authorities that it was Charles who brought the revolver to the meeting, handed it to her, and snarled, "Why don't you kill yourself?" He knocked her to the ground, spat on her, and threatened her with another punch. In a sudden turn of events, she fired the .32 revolver three times, and he dropped to the ground, dead. An autopsy concluded that Patterson died instantly from a bullet that penetrated his back on the left side and pierced his heart. He also took a shot to his right side, two inches below the clavicle.

Hysterical, Gertrude ran through a gate of the Richthofen Castle and screamed, "My husband has committed suicide! Help!" When police arrived she told them, "He had been hitting me and treating me cruelly and I could not stand it any longer so I shot him."

From her jail cell, Gertrude chronicled a life of physical and mental abuse almost from the day they married. "My married life has been one of continual self-defense," she told a reporter.

Gertrude Gibson Patterson went on trial for murder in Denver on November 20. For some, it was "the trial of the century," although an equally high-profile case of infidelity and murder in which two rivals tangled over the favors of Mrs. Isabel "Sassy" Springer, the wife of a prominent Denver businessman, had played out at the historic Brown Palace Hotel the previous May.

Nevertheless, the courthouse on Kalamath Street was jammed with rubberneckers who wanted to get a look at the ravishing Mrs. Patterson and to hear the juicy details of her life between two men. If the court were to convene at 2:30 p.m., men, women, and children lined up at 7 a.m. to secure a seat. The unlucky ones were left to peer in the courtroom windows in the biting cold.

Gertrude recounted numerous occasions when Charles beat her, bit her, and was generally cruel to her.

Trainer Admits Pugilist Is Penniless in England; Anxious to Fight.

Special Cable to the Examiner.
LONDON, Sept. 26.—Jack Johnson is broke. The heavyweight champion, who, after he had whipped Jeffries, quit the ring at Reno a little more than a year ago with $100,000 "to the good" and who has been making money nearly ever since, ap-

Slain Man's Diary Gives Lie Statements in His Divorce Bill.

DENVER, Col., Sept. 26.—A diary kept by Charles A. Patterson, who was shot to death here by his wife after he had sued Emil W. Strauss for alienation of her affections, came to light to-day. Patterson's own handwriting shows that he was aware that his bride, of the months was in Europe with the million manufacturer in January and February 1908, although his complaint filed in Superior Court last Friday set forth that he believed her to have been visiting family in St. Louis during that period. The diary helps support the statement

Patterson as he appeared several years ago in football uniform when he

A former high school football star, Charles Patterson married
Gertrude in 1908 after she became disillusioned with the
much older Emil Strouss. The Patterson marriage was a disaster,
fraught with bouts of drunkenness and physical abuse.

Chicago Examiner

The key defense witness was a surprise. Frank Eaton, a newcomer to town from Wyoming via Tacoma, Washington, told the court that he was out for a walk that day when he reached Twelfth and Oneida Streets, two blocks from the shooting, and noticed the couple arguing.

He said, "The woman was holding a paper. As she handed it back, the man struck her a blow and she staggered. He hit her again and she fell to the ground. Then I heard two shots. The man had his arm raised and appeared like he was going to turn when the shots came and the man pitched forward on his face. After the shooting the woman ran through the gate toward the castle."

He didn't intervene and walked away instead, he said, because "I wanted to keep my foot out of it." Just as mysteriously as he appeared, Eaton disappeared after the trial and efforts to find him were fruitless.

Prosecutor Horace Benson pounded at Gertrude on the witness stand. He dredged up her misadventures as a youngster in Illinois and branded her a "vampire" for living off Strouss and luring Patterson into marriage. He pointed out that despite her contention that she was younger than her late husband she was actually four years older.

Her former lover/benefactor, Emil Strouss, was no help. He wasn't called as a witness and didn't attend the trial. When asked before the trial about his relationship with Gertrude, he told a reporter, "Any statement at this time would not help Mrs. Patterson. She is on trial for murder. So the best thing is silence."

Gertrude was kept in solitary confinement for a time, and then transferred to the main cell with other prisoners. The woman who had lounged in swanky hotels in Chicago and Paris didn't want to room with "common trash," but her request to be given a single cell was rejected.

While she was behind bars she worked on her autobiography, *The Flames of Love*, extracts of which she happily shared with *The Denver Post* through her attorney O. N. Hilton.

> *When I was 16 years old I went with my sister, Mrs. Farnham, and her husband to Chicago. We stopped at the Auditorium Hotel. One day I was introduced to Emil Strouss by a friend of my sister. We grew to be great friends. He was much older than I. At the time I met him my hair was down my back in a braid. He asked me to marry him but said that first I must go to school and study more.*

*After many talks with my people, he finally took me to Paris.
His intentions always seemed to be honorable. We corresponded for
five months then Mr. Strouss wrote me that we would be married before I left Paris. Shortly a cable came to me to return home.
I packed my things and arrived in New York where I found him
waiting for me. We went directly to Chicago, not even waiting
over trains. We went directly to the Grand Pacific Hotel, where Mr.
Strouss registered us as Miss Gibson and Mr. Strouss. The rooms
were adjoining.*

*After this he always agreed to marry me but kept putting it
off. I was so miserable and unhappy, although he gave me everything. The fall of the same year he came for me again. This time he
told me that he had given out information that we were married and that everyone believed it. So we came again to Chicago,
where we stopped at the Stratford Hotel. Mr. Strouss owns part of
that hotel.*

*For five years I lived with Mr. Strouss as his wife. He intro-
duced me as Mrs. Strouss wherever we went and to his friends. No
one ever questioned that I was married to him. For five years I lived
with Mr. Strouss as his wife.*

She described how she met Chick Patterson and the financial arrange-
ments he made with Strouss over her and of her miserable existence
with Patterson and his repeated physical attacks on her. She wanted
Hilton to help her get the book published, but he had to break the news
to her that it was "utterly impossible, not only the English but in the
themes and incidents treated. Much of it would not have been allowed
in the mails and the rest was so poorly told as to defy reconstruction."

The courtroom filled to overflowing on November 30, Thanksgiving
Day, when the jury, which deliberated for seven hours and four ballots,
filed in and took their seats in the jury box. When the bailiff read the
words, "Not guilty," Gertrude gasped and clasped her hands in front
of her as she sprang to her feet. She shook hands with the twelve men
on the jury who had set her free and said, "I believe that I am the very
happiest woman on earth ... and this Thanksgiving Day will be one of the
remembrance of which I shall keep till the end of my days as the happiest

THREE NEW PICTURES OF MRS. GERTRUDE GIBSON PATTERSON

From Photographs by Walinger.

Friend Tells How Strouss
Educated Mrs. Patterson

Reporters who covered her Denver trial in 1911 described
Gertrude Patterson in glowing terms: "Her large brown eyes ⟨have⟩
the softness and innocence of a child's" and "Hers is a doll-like
beauty." The verdict in her murder trial surprised everyone.

Chicago Examiner

one of my life." She even tried to shake prosecutor Benson's hand, but he turned his back on her and walked away.

Despite the judge's preverdict admonishment that no outbursts would be tolerated, the crowd inside and outside the courthouse exploded in cheers. Jurors, some of whom paid a call on Mrs. Patterson at her hotel after the verdict, said it was the evidence, particularly Eaton's sudden testimony, not the defendant's flowerlike face, that led them to vote for acquittal.

Benson was furious. "I think the verdict an outrage and a travesty upon justice."

A backlash from the public against the not-guilty verdict took Gertrude by surprise. Threatening phone calls reached the hotel where she was staying with her family. Petitions were passed to have the verdict overturned. Prominent Reverend H. Martyn Hart, dean of St. John's Cathedral, told a nondenominational gathering of 3,000 at the Auditorium Theater that "the evil communication of this week was corruptive of public morals and so lax a method treating crime endangered the life of every citizen in the community. I am ashamed of the jury for its verdict in this case, and I would be ashamed of myself if I did not cry out against this travesty on righteousness."

Three days after her trial, Gertrude and her entourage, including her beloved dog, Hugo, boarded a train for St. Louis and her parents' home in Sandoval. In one of her last public comments about the shooting and trial she told a correspondent of *The Denver Times* aboard the train carrying her home, "Why can't everyone forget? I am trying to and I am learning to forget it all. I am going to begin a new life and everything that has happened is to be forgotten."

The intervening years have pushed the case into obscurity, but the public's interest did not diminish after she fled Denver. She was said to be living with her parents in Illinois or back in Chicago with Strouss or in her own lush quarters, or in Portland, Oregon, or in Paris or Naples.

In 1912, she was widely reported to have perished in the sinking of the *Titanic* on April 15, which some wags concluded was a well-deserved last act to her life of sin. It wasn't true. She wasn't on the *Titanic* but was instead living in grand style in Chicago, thanks to an anonymous benefactor strongly suspected to be her old friend, Emil W. Strouss. But the one-time lover's fortunes didn't appear to be that grand. According to the 1920 US Census, the former millionaire was living in a South Side apartment building, where his neighbors included retirees, salesmen, a music teacher, and a dentist.

In September 1913, her defense attorney, Hilton, was the last to talk publicly about her life after he visited her in Europe. He told *The Post* that she was living in Paris, having gone straight to Europe after the trial. She was, he said, more beautiful than ever. "She weighs a little more than during the trial. Her cheeks are rosier. ... She was attired in the most marvelous Parisian gown I have ever seen."

CHAPTER 5

THE GOOD WIFE
STELLA MOORE SMITH

She had finally had enough. Two bullets crashing through her brutish husband's skull put a stop to the threats, the coarse language, and the unspeakable insults on her body.

The five hours after midnight on January 13, 1917, seemed to Stella Smith like a nightmare with no awakening. It was the final act in a disastrous marriage that staggered through three years, multiple cities, and a litany of quarrels.

Stella Newton was a shining star of Denver's younger set when she married successful attorney William Moore in an elaborate ceremony at St. Mark's Church on the evening of June 6, 1900. The happy young couple set up housekeeping at 1644 Downing Street and within a few years welcomed a daughter, Mildred.

Moore, whose father, David, was the first chancellor of the University of Denver, was a highly respected member of the city's legal community, a *cum laude* graduate of Columbia University Law School, and a member of the ritzy University Club.

But the prim and conventional life Stella knew fell apart when she fell in love with John Lawrence Smith. She met him in 1910, when he was chauffeur for her stepfather, Alfred Britton, but his advances—and her acceptance of them—didn't bring an end to her marriage to Moore until October 1912.

Smith, thirty-four and three years Stella's senior, was born in Colorado City, where he received little education (she told friends he was barely literate and had to have someone write his letters for him), and, while living in Colorado Springs, he worked as a teamster. He and his first wife, Elizabeth Strauby, had a son, whom they named Herbert. After he and Elizabeth divorced, he moved to Denver, where he found work as a taxi driver before becoming Britton's chauffeur.

Stella married Smith in Yreka, California, on March 24, 1914. A charming, likable—and sober—young man before they wed, he became a raging alcoholic, and transformed into a bully and Stella's millstone after their marriage.

Where Moore was educated and comfortable in society, Smith was rough and headstrong. He rarely worked while he and Stella prowled the country, living on her substantial inheritance from her late stepfather's oil empire. They bounced from Denver to Detroit, Buffalo, Niagara Falls, Portland, Seattle, Sacramento, Berkeley, Oakland, San Francisco, and Los Angeles. They always returned to Denver because that's where Mildred lived with her father.

No matter where the couple lived, the scenario was the same. They fought, Smith beat her, and took money from her. He drank to excess almost around the clock, caroused through bars and brothels, boasted to strangers of his wealth, and returned home to tell Stella about his misbehaviors. She bought him two cars so he could resume his career as a chauffeur; he sold both of them and bought liquor with the money. While they were living in San Francisco in 1915, he told his son, who was traveling with them, "C'mon, we're going to take an auto trip to Seattle. Stella is going to pay for it, but we are going with a new mama."

Stella was a textbook example of an abused wife. She fit the profile almost to the letter—she was fearful that her spouse would hurt her, her daughter, or her ex-husband; she believed that she deserved the abuse; she thought she could control his behavior by doing what he wanted and doing it perfectly. She thought she could fix him. In June 1910, shortly after they met and began their relationship, she wrote to him:

> *Jack, if you will always be like you were yesterday and today, I could love you with all my might. So there! What can I do to keep you like that? And, of course, I was glad to hear your voice over the wire and to know where you were and that you were thinking of me.*
>
> *Wake up, Jack. Don't you know how I want you to be "all well" and how with all my heart I want everything right, so I can love you all I want to and do it happily.*

It was a period when the woman suffrage movement was gathering momentum. On March 3, 1913, an estimated half million spectators, not all of them friendly, watched as 8,000 suffragettes, most of them clad in white, marched from the US Capitol to the White House, demanding of newly reelected President Woodrow Wilson, "How long must women wait for liberty?" The marchers were pelted with cigar butts, spit upon, and generally abused. When America entered World War I in 1917, it freed many women from "their place in the home"; hemlines and tempers rose, but women wouldn't get the constitutional right to vote for another three years.

Stella took a more immediate approach. She would testify at her trial that her unhappy marriage and torturous hell of domestic abuse came to a violent and bloody end in the wee hours of January 13, 1917. Stella and Mildred were living at 4040 Montview Boulevard in the Park Hill neighborhood with their chef, John Bindle, and housekeeper/nanny, Mrs. Mary Greenhill, when there was a knock on the front door at 2 a.m. Bindle, thinking it was a telegram delivery, opened the door and in barged a very drunk John Smith.

He swept past Bindle and bounded up the stairs to Stella's second-floor bedroom, where she and her daughter, twelve-year-old Mildred, were sharing a bed. Smith silently crossed the bedroom and touched Stella's shoulder without speaking. Startled, she quickly put on a robe and led him to the adjoining sitting room so Mildred wouldn't hear their conversation. "He isn't fit to be in the presence of her; his every word is blasphemy," she would say later.

During the couple's intense conversation, she told Bindle to go downtown and bring her ex-husband to the house so he could take Mildred away. She could tell Smith had been drinking; she had seen it enough times. Reaching into his coat pocket, he produced a pint of whiskey, took several pulls on it, and ordered her to drink. She refused. With that, he took out his revolver, laid it over his arm and said, "You will drink it." She took a sip.

Their argument woke Mildred, and Stella ordered her to go sleep in the sitting room. Fearing for her mother, she came back into the room and Stella scolded her. "Mildred, go back to bed." Smith chimed in, "Yes, go get into bed and I will be in there in a minute and get into bed with you."

He commanded Stella to take off every stitch of clothing she had on and do the "jelly wobble" on her hands and knees. She pleaded that she didn't know that particular dance but she sensed he wanted her to crawl around on the floor. She hesitated. He became violent and tore off her bathrobe and nightgown. While she was down on all fours, he "sought to commit a heinous and atrocious and unnatural action upon her," as her attorney delicately described it to the jury.

To keep him at bay she pretended to be sick from the small amount of whiskey she had consumed, but he insisted that she drink more. When she didn't, he poured the remainder of the bottle over her naked body, then left to use the bathroom.

When he got back, she later testified at a coroner's inquest, "He tried to get some sign of life from me; he pulled the hair on my body and he pulled the nipples nearly out of my breasts." This time, she was ready for him. Grabbing her .22-caliber revolver from beneath her pillow, she closed her eyes and from her knees fired a single shot. He fell backward to the floor.

Panicked, she threw on a blanket and ran downstairs to get Bindle, who had heard the shot and was coming up. She led him into the bedroom to show him what she had done, and then she thought she saw Smith twitch. Fearing he was still alive, she grabbed his gun, clutched his hair with her left hand, put the muzzle of his .38 close to his face, and fired a single shot.

Taken to the city jail, Stella Smith professed no regret. Newspaper reporters enjoyed extraordinary access to her and she repeated her version of the shooting over and over. "I'm glad," she said to a *Denver Post* reporter. "I'm glad I killed him. I don't care what they do with me. You might ask why I stood such persecution for three years. I stood it because I feared the man. I feared for my own life and for the lives of my daughter and my former husband. When he was drunk he was a pervert of the most degraded type. I had to submit to horrors which you could not publish in your newspaper."

Dr. Ward Burdick, the city's pathologist, testified at the inquest that either of the gunshots would have meant instant death for Smith. The bullet from her .22 entered his head on the right side, just behind the temple, and ranged upward and backward in his skull. Stella delivered the second bullet when Smith was lying on his back on the bedroom floor. Burdick said at the hearing that he found a discoloration on the right upper eyelid, a hole through the right cheek, and powder burns on his face.

SATURDAY, JANUARY 13, 1917   The Wise Market Basket Brigade Shops T

I SHOT TO SAVE THE HONOR OF MY CHILD, I'M SATISFIED, DECLARES STELLA SMITH

PRINCIPALS IN THIS MORNING'S MURDER IN THE FASHIONABLE RESIDENCE DISTRICT OF PARK HILL

Stella Smith's second husband, left, was a drunken abuser
who freely spent her inheritance. When she married her
first husband, William Moore, below, in 1900, it was
regarded as the society wedding of the year.

The Denver Post, courtesy of the Western History and Genealogy Department, Denver Public Library

Smith's body lay unclaimed for three days in the coroner's cooler. Stella said, "I wouldn't bury the dog that bit me," but she did. She paid his funeral expenses, but there is no headstone on his grave at Riverside Cemetery.

Mrs. Smith's trial began on March 17. District Attorney William Foley, in charge of the prosecution, was of two minds about putting Stella on trial for the murder of an abusive husband. He called the killing "wanton and cold-blooded" but declined to ask for the death penalty, choosing to leave that up to the jury.

One of her defense attorneys, Howard Honan, countered that she did it not only to protect herself from bodily injury but also to protect her body from being befouled. Self-defense, plain and simple.

Will Moore, the ex-husband, stood by her. He brought their daughter to visit Stella in her jail cell. "I have the deepest sympathy for her and I feel that the shooting was justified," he told the newspapers. "The only thing I blame myself for is that I didn't kill Smith myself instead of letting the poor woman do it. If any man deserved to die, it was he. He was a worthless wretch."

Trying to spare the public the salacious details, Judge John W. Sheafor ordered that there be no spectators in his court during the defense's portion of the trial. On the fourth day, Stella Smith took the witness stand. The *Rocky Mountain News* reporter described her in meticulous detail: "Mrs. Smith smiled when her name was called and, rising quickly, walked firmly, head up, to the stand. She was clad in a black velvet skirt, black net [shirt] waist over dark blue with a large white collar. Across one shoulder was a flung a handsome black fur. Her only jewelry was a necklace of small gold beads."

In a firm and unwavering voice, she repeated the events of January 13 and reeled off numerous abuses Smith brought down on her during their marriage. She told how he became enraged one night because dinner wasn't ready. "He took the roast from the oven and stamped on it." They fought on the train en route to Chicago. He tried to strangle her at Niagara Falls.

To *The Post*, she revealed the torment of their tumultuous life together. "All that Smith seemed to want of me except when he was drunk was money, money, money."

There was one damaging bit of evidence brought up by the prosecutor. Several employees of the Oxford Hotel testified that Mrs. Smith

The 1917 murder trial of Stella Newton Smith was so salacious, the presiding judge ordered her testimony barred from the public. Stella was the object of repeated sexual abuse by her chauffeur-husband. Fed up, she shot him, then shot him again to make sure he was dead. She was acquitted.

The Denver Post, courtesy of the Western History and Genealogy Department, Denver Public Library

registered at the hotel as "Mrs. Charles Miller, Detroit, Mich." on January 11, two nights before the murder, and met her husband there, proving, said the prosecution, that she didn't fear him all that much. The night clerk later said he was "mistaken" and the woman he saw was, in fact, not Stella Smith, but Mrs. Ross C. Brown, visiting from Detroit.

The prosecution had no other ammunition. It became clear to observers that there was no chance of a conviction.

At 12:01 p.m. on Friday, March 30, the twelve-man jury sat down to review the testimony and other evidence and talk about their options, ranging from first-degree murder with the death penalty to acquittal. They were in the jury room only thirteen minutes and took one, unanimous vote. When they reassembled in the courtroom, foreman Frank Varnum passed their decision to the court clerk, who read it and passed it back. "Not guilty," he said.

The courtroom erupted in cheers and applause. Stella gave out a combination of a laugh and a sob. Women rushed past the bailiff to surround her. As the throng patted and hugged her she said, "I can't tell you how grateful I am. I just can't tell you. You've made me happy again. I can go home now, home to my little girl."

She was taken directly to 4040 Montview and the long-awaited reunion with Mildred. During the time in her jail cell, she promised that if she were acquitted and once Mildred was out of school, they would leave Denver for a visit with friends in the East. She did just that. On June 13, a want ad in *The Post* offered, "10-room modern house for rent, furnished for 3 or 6 months. 2 sleeping porches, garden, lawn and trees." In December 1921 she put 4040 up for sale and a similar ad said, "Owner has left city permanently and is anxious to sell."

Stella Newton Moore—she would reclaim her previous name in 1918—the woman who endured a hellish experience with a fiendish husband and a trial in which her most private secrets were made pubic, moved to West Point, New York, during World War I. She moved back to Denver in 1948, once again to be close to Mildred, and died at her home at 1572 Fillmore Street, on April 10, 1951, at age seventy-seven.

She and her ex-husband, William, who died of pneumonia on April 20, 1925, one day before his sixty-first birthday, are buried a few yards apart in Fairmount Cemetery.

CHAPTER 6

THE ROADHOUSE ROBBERY

IRENE NOLAN

"Stick 'em up, up, up!"

The couple, startled by gunshots fired into the floor of the private dining room, at first thought it had to be a joke but obligingly put up their hands. The masked bandit ordered the man to empty his pockets and shouted at the woman to hand over her diamond rings. "Come through with them or I'll kill you!"

Just as quickly as he had appeared, the robber fled out the front door of the Model Roadhouse and into the early morning darkness. The stickup turned out to be much more than a run-of-the-mill crime because it would snare a society woman, her priest, and a Denver detective in a web that titillated the public for weeks.

On January 1, 1918, Father Garrett Burke, the priest at Holy Ghost Catholic Church in downtown Denver, decided to ring in the new year by making house calls on his flock. It was getting late in the day and he was tired, but he decided on one more stop, at the apartment of his friend and parishioner Irene Nolan, 1276 Corona Street. It was after 11 p.m. by the time he reached her door, but she was still awake and in a mood to celebrate, even though her husband, Harry, was out of town on business. She liked to party.

Irene Nolan
The Denver Post, courtesy of the Western History and Genealogy Department, Denver Public Library

Mrs. Nolan was twenty-nine, dark haired, dark eyed, and attractive, with a reputation as a "butterfly" around the Denver clubs. She was seventeen years younger than her husband, a highly successful businessman, one of the first motion-picture theater operators in the United States, and a pioneer in Hollywood movie production. His far-flung empire took him to California, Utah, Montana, and other western states, and, concerned about his wife's amusements while he was out of town, he turned to Father Burke as a "spiritual advisor."

In Nolan's absence, Father Burke's assignment was to try to keep Mrs. Nolan out of trouble. Her husband told Father Burke that he didn't feel he could take her about as much as she would like. The priest promised Harry that he would do everything in his power to dissuade Mrs. Nolan from her inclinations.

Mrs. Nolan and Father Burke chatted and shared a bottle of champagne. Then they had another bottle of champagne, and that's when Irene decided it was a splendid night for a drive, out where there was "a million dollars worth of air." The two got into the priest's car, which was having mechanical problems, and motored about seven miles north of town. The balky auto sputtered in front of the Model Roadhouse close to 2 a.m., so they went in to telephone for help.

The barroom was crowded. Among the patrons were Philip Cohen and Frank Mulligan, who would play major roles in the drama about to unfold.

They were all drunk. In the dark days during Prohibition, the Model Roadhouse, far out in the country on Brighton Boulevard near today's Interstate 270, was a popular playground for dining, dancing, and drinking. It was considered a more upscale alternative to the roughneck Hiawatha Roadhouse a few blocks away. Prohibition, which took effect in Colorado in 1916, didn't deter a thirsty citizenry. There were plenty of places like the Model and the Hiawatha to take your liquor and get "setups," nonalcoholic mixers.

When the couple arrived at the roadhouse, they were greeted at the door by Jake Fineberg, who ran the place, and were led around to a side entrance into a private dining room off the barroom, where the three chatted and "drank pop," Father Burke told police. Each of them may have had one drink, Mrs. Nolan said.

Waiter Harry Schuenberg told a different story. He thought they were both "pretty well liquored up" when they arrived. He served them

Much younger than her husband, Harry, Irene Nolan was
a free-spirited "butterfly" who went on a late-night drinking
spree with her family priest and wound up the victim of
a diamond robbery at an Adams County speakeasy.
Rocky Mountain News, courtesy of the Western History and Genealogy Department, Denver Public Library

repeated rounds of ginger ale and Manitou water, but, he added, he was pretty sure they had liquor too. "I expect they did. Every time I brought clean glasses in and took the other ones out, they smelled of liquor from somewhere." He brought them "about ten" setups.

When 3 a.m. rolled around, Fineberg said he was going home and suggested that Mrs. Nolan and her companion do the same. They refused. Mrs. Nolan said they were going to have breakfast, then drive to Cheyenne. Fineberg, the staff, and musicians left the couple as the lone patrons. Mulligan and Cohen, who had been at the roadhouse earlier in the evening, went back to Denver, then returned in the early hours.

At 5:30 a.m., the front door burst open and in rushed an armed man, later identified as Cohen, while his cohort waited outside. He went immediately to Father Burke and Mrs. Nolan with his command, "Stick 'em up, up, up!" The priest, swearing he had no cash, obediently laid his watch on the table. The thief declined it, demanding the seven diamond rings Mrs. Nolan had on her fingers, which were worth approximately $3,000 (about $42,000 today).

Chaos reigned in the aftermath. Hysterical, Mrs. Nolan cried, "My diamonds! My diamonds! Oh, what will Harry do? I must tell Harry all about it." She said to Burke, "Why didn't you save my diamonds for me?" to which he responded with a shrug, "How could I save them when the fellow had a gun on me?" Someone poured her a whiskey. Panicked, she called Fineberg at the Orient Hotel in Denver to ask what she should do. Friends with both Mrs. Nolan and Father Burke, Fineberg hurried back to the roadhouse but declined later to reveal their names to police because "it would cause a scandal."

After the incident, Father Burke left town and was variously reported to be in Texas, Salt Lake City, Kansas City, Florida, and Louisville, Kentucky. He eventually returned to testify in the two holdup men's trials. He wasn't defrocked by the church but lost his parish at Holy Ghost, replaced by a young priest named William Neenan.

After leaving the roadhouse that night, Mulligan caught a ride back to his Denver home at 3033 West Bosler Place, where he was greeted by Effie, his unamused wife. "He was drunk [when he got home]. He couldn't hardly walk, his eyes were bleary and he went to bed with his clothes on." She spared him a lecture. "What's the use of talking to a drunken man?"

Fineberg gave Mrs. Nolan a ride home to her apartment in mid-morning, where she prepared to tell Harry "all about it." After his return from his business trip to Salt Lake City, Harry Nolan held both his wife and Father Burke blameless. "Of course," he told the press, "it was indiscreet and regrettable but that is something that can't be helped."

Four days after the holdup, arrest warrants were issued for Philip Cohen and Frank Mulligan. It was no great surprise since both men were known to Fineberg and were seen at the Model the night of the crime. Mulligan, forty-one, was a detective and fourteen-year veteran of the Denver Police Department. After the incident, he went to Chief Hamilton Armstrong, and cleansed his conscience:

> *I have made an ass of myself, chief, and I have come to you to admit it. I was at the roadhouse. I went out there with a man named Kerrigan and Tommy Bartless. They had a couple of bottles of whisky and I got drunk. It was the first time in a year that I have been under the influence of liquor. I can't stand whisky and I know it, and for that reason I generally let it alone but this time I allowed it to get the best of me.*
>
> *While I was out there I fired four shots into the floor from my revolver. I didn't know what I was doing. I didn't know that Father Burke or Mrs. Nolan were there. Robbery was the farthest thing from my mind. In fact, I was too drunk to plan or carry out a robbery if I chose to do so.*

He denied any direct involvement in the holdup, but he was charged with conduct unbecoming an officer of the law and suspended from the force.

Two weeks later, Mrs. Nolan's stolen diamonds mysteriously reappeared, mailed to a Denver jewelry store from a fake address in Pueblo. The robbers—Mulligan devised the plan and Cohen carried it out—were sure that Mrs. Nolan and Father Burke would not report the robbery because of their prominence in Denver and the awkward circumstances of their night on the town, apparently believing that once the diamonds were returned, the charges would be dropped.

That's not how it played out. Mulligan and Cohen went on trial in district court in Adams County for grand larceny in March 1918. Mul-

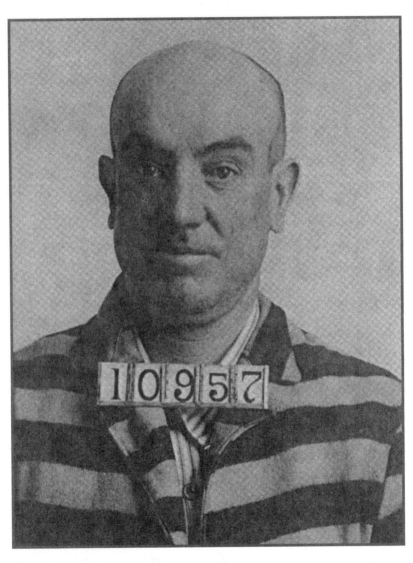

Denver police detective Frank Mulligan told a judge he could
not have taken part in the Model Roadhouse stickup
because he was "too drunk to carry out a robbery."
He served five years in the station penitentiary for grand larceny.
Courtesy of the Colorado State Archives

ligan maintained his innocence in the holdup, but others placed him at the door of the roadhouse after the robbery. Despite Mulligan's confession to Chief Armstrong that he was the one who fired the shots at the Model, Father Burke and Mrs. Nolan identified Cohen as the stickup man. "Yes, that's the man," she said firmly. "There is no doubt about it." Identifying him wasn't that difficult—the diminutive Cohen stood only five-foot-five and had a noticeable scar on his nose. Besides, the kerchief covering his face slipped down during the holdup.

Mrs. Nolan was not a very effective witness. She wept and moaned while under questioning by the defense attorney during Mulligan's trial. She told attorney John W. Gillespie that she couldn't remember a lot of the details of that night. Gillespie tore into her during his summation: "These people [Father Burke and Mrs. Nolan] are a pair of renegades in society. How would you like to have that woman for a wife? Think of this idea: This priest leaving the home of a married woman, when her husband was away, to go out and get some fresh air and then going to the hog pens and cattle pens in the stockyards [near the roadhouse]. They did not drive out in the parks and boulevards where there were lights."

After a week of testimony, Mulligan and Cohen were sentenced by Judge Harry S. Class to five to seven years, the minimum sentence for robbery with a gun. Mulligan put his head down and wept openly. He told the court to "do its worst. There has been good teamwork here. I have received about as raw a deal in your court as a man ever received in a court of justice! ... But I don't expect leniency from this kangaroo court. But you wanted to 'job' me! I'm no quitter and no dog. Now, shoot your lump and put an end to this extravaganza performance!" When it came his turn, Cohen said nothing.

Cohen and Mulligan, partners in crime, were received at the state prison at Cañon City on April 14, 1920, and both were pardoned by Governor Oliver Shoup on May 26, 1922, having served two years of their five-year sentence on top of the two years they were behind bars in the Adams County jail.

Despite the publicity surrounding the Model Roadhouse affair, the Nolans remained married until she died of a heart attack at her home, 770 Clarkson Street, in 1936 when she was forty-eight years old.

After his release from prison, Mulligan worked various jobs, including as a salesman and an electrician, until he dropped dead while working at the Selective Service board office in Denver on September 3, 1942. He and his wife, Effie, who divorced him in 1931, are buried side by side at Riverside Cemetery, ironically not a mile from the location of the Model Roadhouse.

CHAPTER 7

THE DEATH OF A SALESMAN

J. FRANKLIN RENFRO

J. Franklin Renfro was literally running for his life before his would-be
assassin cornered him behind a stranger's bungalow in North Denver.
His right arm thrown up in a futile effort to protect his face, Renfro
pleaded for mercy.

A man believed to be ex-convict Jesse McDaniel, the cuckolded
husband of Renfro's lover, was having none of it. "Get up!" he shouted.
"Get up! Get out of there!" Enraged, he emptied his .25-caliber automat-
ic into the terrified thirty-eight-year-old real-estate salesman cowering
a mere five feet from him. Renfro died almost instantly from devastating
wounds to his abdomen, pancreas, and right lung on September 16, 1919.

Denver in the late teens was in turmoil. Controversial mayor
Robert Speer was voted out of office by reformers opposed to his *lais-
sez-faire* attitude toward the city's vices, then voted back in; World War
I, which ended in November 1918, produced a frenzy of high patriotism
when Coloradans with German surnames were suspected of being spies;
a postwar real-estate boom and rapidly rising food prices squeezed the
average Coloradan. On top of it all, the worldwide flu epidemic appeared
and disappeared in Colorado several times between September 1918 and
June 1919, killing hundreds.

J. Frankliin Renfro

Courtesy private collection

Nevertheless, Renfro's murder was page-one news in both local papers. "ASSASSIN LURES REALTY MAN TO DEATH" shouted a banner headline in all capitals across the top of page one of *The Denver Post*. The *Rocky Mountain News* was no less bombastic: "City Realty Salesman Assassinated." Both papers devoted long stories and numerous photographs to the steamy tale of love and betrayal.

Police immediately dubbed the murder "a woman affair." They were dead-on. Renfro had been keeping company with McDaniel's wife, Adda, for some time; their affair began a year earlier when both lived in Cheyenne, Wyoming.

The killing was carefully orchestrated. Earlier in the day, Renfro received a phone call at his desk at J. H. Wilkins Realty and scribbled a short note to himself: "Mr. Gilpin/4585 Vrain Street/6:45 p.m./to sell 3815 Wolff Street." It was like many other leads he received, but this one was a sham—the Wolff Street address was a house owned by Wilkins Realty and there was no "Mr. Gilpin."

Eager to make a sale, Renfro left his office at 615 Seventeenth Street and, as he went out the door, predicted out loud that he would sell the Wolff Street property. "Don't come back unless you do," joked his boss. Renfro hurried through dinner, and went to the Wynne Hotel, a few blocks away at 1431 California Street, where he had been living since he and his wife, Alice, separated in May. For reasons known only to him, Renfro invited Robert Harris, night clerk at the Wynne, to "take a ride to the North Side," and bring his wife, Jean. A fifteen-minute drive brought them to the front of the house at 4585 Vrain, where a stranger, apparently interested in buying a property, walked up to the car and said to Renfro, "Let's walk down this way." The Harrises stayed in the car while the two men strolled down the street and cut through a potato patch toward Winona Court, the next street west.

Things deteriorated within minutes. Both men began gesticulating and talking heatedly. Walking slightly behind Renfro, his assailant shouted, "Go on, you go on!" and whacked him on the head with a wooden club hidden inside a rolled-up newspaper. Renfro staggered and ran for cover. As he scurried behind the house on Winona Court, a block from where the chase started, he yelled back, "Go easy! Go easy!" He frantically tried to open the screen door but a faulty latch wouldn't budge. He was trapped. Bullets tore into his body—police estimated he suffered ten wounds, including a shot that went through his wrist and into his

Three of the principals in the tangled personal affairs and shooting death of J. Franklin Renfro, clockwise from top: Jesse McDaniel, Alice Renfro, and J. Franklin Renfro.

The Denver Post, courtesy of the Western History and Genealogy Department, Denver Public Library

mouth—and he crumpled to the ground. A coroner's jury concluded that he died from wounds "inflicted by some unknown person with felonious intent." McDaniel was not mentioned.

The sound of gunfire alerted neighbors, who hurried to the scene and tried vainly to grab the shooter, but he scaled a backyard fence and ran down the alley between Wolff and Xavier to Forty-Sixth Street, where he fled in a stolen car parked nearby. Police scoured the neighborhood near Berkeley Park but never found him. His getaway was clean.

After the shooting, police located Renfro's wife, Alice, at the Denham Theater, located at Eighteenth and California Streets downtown, where she was enjoying the Wilkes Players' production—"glistening with comedy"— of "A Small Town Girl." When they told her her husband was dead, she said simply, "I expected it! I expected it."

She had no doubt that "Mrs. Adda McDaniel is behind this thing. My husband has tried his best to get away from her but [she] has repeatedly threatened to kill both of us. It got so he was afraid to be seen with me for fear of her. But for this woman my husband and myself would not have had any trouble."

If Renfro was trying to extricate himself from the welcoming arms of Mrs. McDaniel, he wasn't doing much of a job of it. He did ask for police protection in Cheyenne because he was afraid Adda would shoot him. In April 1918, he moved his family to Denver—to get away from her, he said—but it wasn't long before he and Adda reconnected. A fellow employee at the real estate office recalled that Renfro had been in the company of Mrs. McDaniel "a great deal of the time" but assumed it was a purely business relationship. Things were heating up as early as May. Someone slipped a note under the door of Renfro's home. "Mrs. Renfro," it read, "if you will call York 3737 I can tell you who the lady is I see your husband with. Don't think you are the only woman he had." Franklin Renfro called the number, listed to the Florence Apartments on Washington Street, trying to find out who might have sent the note. Elizabeth Reuss, the janitor's wife, had no idea, but added, "He was excited about the affair and was eager to straighten it out." Eager, because "[Alice] is the finest woman I know," he said. "I don't want her to leave me but she certainly will unless this thing can be stopped."

Alice and Franklin married in 1912 in Nebraska, moved to Cheyenne, and then to Denver in 1918. It was his third marriage; he had two daughters and a son from his second. While they lived in Cheyenne, his business and his marriage were good. He sold insurance and ran a brokerage in oil stocks, making him one of the state's leading businessmen, according to his profile in *History of Wyoming*. He was, said his profile, "a man of unfaltering enterprise and unabating energy."

The presumed shooter was born Jesse F. McDaniel (*The Denver Post* repeatedly referred to him as "MacDaniel" but census and other records spelled it "McDaniel") in Kentucky in 1880. Witnesses to the Denver shooting described him as slightly built, about five-foot-nine and 150 pounds with "an athletic build."

As a young man, he bounced around from Kentucky to Ohio to Pennsylvania to Wyoming before his arrest as a car thief and sentencing to prison in April 1917. In May 1917, he escaped from Pennsylvania's New Western Penitentiary (later renamed Rockview Penitentiary), where he was serving a two-year sentence for grand larceny and receiving stolen goods. Prison officials labeled him "an inveterate gambler, a diamond switcher, a clever confidence man ... is quite widely known to the sporting fraternity."

He and Adda were married in Beaver, Pennsylvania, in 1903. They had two daughters and by 1910 they were living in Laramie, Wyoming, where he found work driving a truck.

McDaniel made his 1917 prison escape stick, and by 1918, he was again living with his wife in Cheyenne. Cheyenne is also where Mrs. McDaniel sought insurance advice, and something more, from Franklin Renfro. Adda, thirty-nine, was tall and strikingly good looking, with dark, smoldering eyes. She soon was smitten with the rising young businessman who had better prospects than her vagabond husband.

After the shooting, Adda refused to cooperate with the police investigation. In fact, she was downright hostile. When they barged into her Bannock Street apartment at 1 a.m. the night of the killing, she wasn't helpful. "What authority have you to come here and wake me up at this time of night?" She remained defiant: "I'm not interested in the opinion of a world that has robbed me of the only man I care for. [This] is my own particular affair and nobody else's."

In the days following the murder, *The Post*'s Frances "Pinky" Wayne, the newspaper's "sob sister" specializing in stories about abused wives and

J. Franklin Renfro moved from Cheyenne to Denver
with his wife, Alice, and his two daughters, Gladys, left,
and Alvena, to avoid future confrontations with his
extramarital affinity, Adda McDaniel. It didn't work.

Courtesy private collection

orphaned children, interviewed both men's wives. Her reporting made it clear that she did not approve of the home wrecker Adda. Wayne huffed that Adda McDaniel "is as tempered steel to swan's down … dominant, hard, self-reliant, detached." Wayne found her living in a rooming house near today's Civic Center: "She lay on the couch in the half-shadowed room cluttered with wearing apparel, shoes, slippers, and the paraphernalia which indicates disorderliness."

Her sympathies lay with the wronged wife, Alice Renfro, whom Wayne described as having "a white girlish throat … her blond head … hazel eyes set in a face with an upturned nose, round trembling chin and creamy complexion." She listened patiently as Alice told how Adda McDaniel stalked her husband in Cheyenne.

"Two years ago my husband and I were at dinner, talking in a friendly way, when the door suddenly opened and a woman walked into the home. 'You'll give that woman up and come to me or I'll do some killing,' she screamed at my husband and pointed to me, and for the first time I knew he had hidden something from me."

As day follows night, the repercussion was immediate. "I asked what it meant and my husband told me that the woman was Mrs. McDaniel, whom he had met in a business transaction." No sale. "We had a long talk over the affair when the woman left the house. I was too hurt to be angry because I always believed my husband loved me," Alice told Wayne. "I suggested that perhaps the best thing to be done was for me to return to my father's house in Nebraska until he could straighten [things] out with the woman."

She believed he was serious about saving their marriage, and he said he was, promising her that once the clouds parted they could patch things up. The family fled to Denver, where she ended up living with her brother-in-law Charles Fennel at 832 Twenty-Eighth Street after the couple's separation. "I knew he was suffering under the conditions in which he found himself," she said. "I knew he wanted to be free of the woman who not only had broken into our home but broken it up."

Mrs. McDaniel scoffed at Alice's tale of being terrorized in her own home. "As for the story of his wife's that I threatened their lives, it is absolutely false. I would never be fool enough for that."

Called in a second time for two and a half hours of questioning by Police Chief Hamilton Armstrong, Adda complained,

Mr. Armstrong sent for me in an automobile and I went to the police station at once as I thought that maybe he had some information that I might be able to help him on. When I got there he began to cross-question me and kept it up until 5 o'clock. He was very rude to me and threatened to throw me in jail. God knows that I am as anxious that [the killer] be arrested as anybody because Mr. Renfro was a good friend of mine.

The police seem to think I am trying to hold back something from them. Well, I'm not for if I knew anything I'll swear before God that I would tell them if it would help them locate this man who killed Mr. Renfro. I know nothing about where he is. He is the father of my daughters and I still have a warm spot in my heart for him.

Numerous questions about the case remain unanswered. How, for example, did Renfro not recognize the man who approached his car in front of the Vrain Street property? In July, *The Post* reported, Renfro and a coworker were walking downtown after lunch when Renfro spied a familiar face walking toward them. "Here comes McDaniel," he told his coworker. "Let's go behind this car until he goes by."

And, three hours before their fatal confrontation in North Denver on September 16, witnesses said Renfro and a man resembling McDaniel were involved in a brief fight at Seventeenth and California Streets near Renfro's office over $500 McDaniel demanded from the real estate man.

Also unanswered is where the money came from that Adda used to buy two apartment houses—with Renfro's help—in the summer of 1918. She spent $4,500 to buy a rooming house at 1369 Bannock Street and $7,000 for an apartment building at 1543 Steele Street. Renfro thought the money came from her husband's bootlegging, but police in Greeley, a town in northern Colorado, pegged McDaniel as a suspect in a post office robbery in which $10,000 in Liberty bonds had been stolen.

Three days after the shooting, police theorized that McDaniel was planning to set sail with his family to South America. To McDaniel's dismay, Adda had spent the money he gave her for the tickets to buy the two apartment houses. "When he found that I had bought property with the money and the Liberty bonds he gave me, he was very upset," she told police.

McDaniel must have left Denver before July 1924 because his wife was granted a divorce that year on grounds of desertion. In fact, he probably left soon after the murder because, she said, she hadn't seen him in four years.

There was one more bit of drama to be played out in Adda's life: In April 1971, Adda was injured when a would-be mugger tried to snatch her purse on East Colfax Avenue.

She died in 1971 in Colorado Springs age eighty-seven. Franklin and Alice were finally reunited fifty years after the murder, when she died in 1969 and was buried beside her husband at Denver's Fairmount Cemetery.

The pursuit of McDaniel heated up again in February 1925 when police in Alexandria, Louisiana, wired Denver's Captain of Detectives Washington Rinker, saying they had arrested a man answering McDaniel's description on charges of bigamy and "feel sure he is the man you want."

Denver police sent Jesse's fingerprints, photographs, and Bertillon measurements (a once widely used series of body measurements used to identify a suspect) with two detectives to take a look at the Louisiana suspect; it never came to anything. The chances that it was McDaniel are slim. The man—whose name on the Louisiana arrest record is "Jessie McDaniels"—was being held for bigamy with five wives and was born in Ohio; McDaniel was born in Kentucky.

Jesse McDaniel, whom everyone involved believed coldly executed J. Franklin Renfro, was never found.

CHAPTER 8

THE BUCKET OF BLOOD

FREDERICK BONFILS

Frederick Gilmer Bonfils was a man blessed with luck and fueled by a burning ambition for wealth.

He was regarded as one of Denver's best-looking men; only William F. "Buffalo Bill" Cody drew more compliments. Athletically built and a dedicated outdoorsman, Bonfils had dark hair that curled down over his forehead, light-blue eyes, and a never-ending drive to get rich.

"[He was] a watchdog over his bankroll, believing that money meant Power and Power was God Almighty," wrote Gene Fowler in *Timber Line*, his romping history of *The Denver Post*. Robert Perkin in *The First Hundred Years*, his history of Denver and its newspapers, described Bonfils in more detail: "Above a magnificently groomed and waxed mustache, the nose was patrician, ever so slightly aquiline. The manner was reserved, lofty, and regal, and Bonfils strode the earth like a conqueror."

But he also called Bonfils "a strange and contradictory man, [who] wanted to be liked by the city he plundered. He parlayed the luck and insight into great wealth and a power probably greater than that of any other man in Denver's history. Yet many wondered if Fred Bonfils found his prizes satisfying."

His lust for riches eventually swept him up in the famed Teapot Dome oil scandal, one of the nation's sleaziest.

Bonfils arrived in Denver in 1895 with a background that could charitably be described as "colorful." As a young reporter for the *Troy* (MO) *News*, he once decked a gatekeeper for refusing him admission to the state fair. It was a portent of things to come. He dropped out of the US Military Academy at West Point in 1881 after he was set back a year because of "a deficiency in mathematics," ironic for a man who became known as a penny-pincher and kept meticulous track of every loan and debt.

In 1886, he moved to Kansas City and began dealing in real estate. He saw opportunity in the 1889 homesteading rush in the Oklahoma Territory and launched the first of a series of schemes when he bought a section of land on the Texas side of the border with Oklahoma and advertised lots in Oklahoma City, Texas. "Oklahoma City" appeared large in advertisements with "Texas" in tiny letters below. The land was miles from water and there was no railroad serving the square mile of sagebrush and scrub oak. He peddled five thousand lots for $2 to $2.25, pocketing $15,000 before authorities shut down the fraud.

This was a temporary setback. Shortly after, he turned his attention to a popular form of gambling—lotteries. Operating under various names in Kansas City, Kansas, including L. E. Winn, Eli Little, and the Little Louisiana Lottery Company, he reaped more than $100,000 in profits from lotteries in which almost no one won. He was arrested twice, once for "loitering around a lottery" and once for "conducting a lottery," paid minimal fines, and beat it out of town.

His life changed when he met his eventual partner in *The Post*, Harry Tammen, in a Chicago hotel. Tammen, working as a bartender at the posh Windsor Hotel in Denver, wanted to buy the moribund *Post* but needed a backer. Bonfils was the perfect target. Armed with Bonfils's $12,500, the two men bought *The Post* on October 28, 1895, when Bonfils was thirty-four and Tammen thirty-nine.

It was the start of a spectacular journalistic circus. Robert Perkin observed, "Denver was amazed, startled, fascinated, and left waiting, slack-jawed, to see what *The Post* would pull next." It was a wild ride, featuring big red headlines, scandals, and head-scratching stories like "Does It Hurt to Be Born?" While neither man knew the first thing about managing a newspaper, Bonfils's advice to Tammen was, "Write the news for all the people, not just the rich and important or those who think they are. If you are understood by the busy, simple folks, everybody will understand you. And always remember—we want people to talk about *The Post*."

And talk they did, thanks in part to an endless string of promotions—treasure hunts, oldest married couple, biggest trout, best-shaped foot, and cooking schools, to name a few—all at no expense to the paper. They even owned a real-life circus, the Sells Floto. But, as Fowler pointed out, "Underneath all their circus-like activities, *The Post* owners were shrewd businessmen. They made sure of giving the sucker more news and more excitement and more features than it was possible for any competitor to do. That practice guaranteed circulation, and circulation guaranteed advertising."

The two men could not have been more different. Bonfils was private, austere—a man with few close confidants (his nearest close friend was his bodyguard and court jester Volney Hoggatt)—and tightfisted. He once told Tammen, "It only spoils a man to overpay him, to give him something he doesn't deserve."

Tammen, on the other hand, was short, roly-poly, fun loving, a showman, and bursting with promotional ideas. He shunned the outdoor life, preferring the comforts of home. Recalling his mother's words, he signed all his letters, "With love and good cheer."

Propelled by publicity-generating promotions, the paper's circulation grew quickly. Along with it grew the two men's power in Denver—power they wielded to land advertisers.

The men's success—and their brand of fire-wagon journalism—did not endear them to their competitors or to the businessmen and other public figures they regularly skewered in print. The *Rocky Mountain News* called its rival "that blackmailing, blackguarding, nauseous sheet which stinks to high heaven and which is the shame of newspapermen the world over." A politician whom they crossed complained in a speech before civic leaders at the Brown Palace Hotel, "F. G. Bonfils is a public enemy and has left the trail of a slimy serpent across Colorado for thirty years."

Bonfils was a man of Corsican temperament, and these types of attacks did not pass unnoticed. During the holiday season in 1907, he overtook *News* publisher Thomas Patterson at East Thirteenth Avenue and Logan Street as both men were walking to work. "Good morning," said Bonfils. When Patterson turned to him, Bonfils decked the sixty-seven-year-old Patterson with a series of punches.

It would not be the volatile Bonfils's last such run-in. Six years later, he came to blows with Thomas O'Donnell, an attorney for the Water Department—the same department that was working to renew its franchise

Driven by a lust for power and wealth, Frederick Bonfils, co-owner
of *The Denver Post*, ran afoul of the federal government in
1924 when he became enmeshed in the Teapot Dome scandal
investigation. He denied his paper quit attacking the leases
after a secret agreement with oilman Harry Sinclair.

Courtesy of *The Denver Post*

with the city of Denver, a deal that *The Post* opposed. Bonfils said O'Donnell pulled a gun on him before he unleashed a right hand. O'Donnell said he showed the weapon only after Bonfils's attack.

The wildest physical encounter, however, took place in December 1899 in the Red Room, also known as the "Bucket of Blood"—the red-hued offices Bonfils and Tammen shared at *The Post*. As one of its high-profile crusades, *The Post* helped free man-eater Alfred Packer, who was serving forty years in the Colorado State Penitentiary for cannibalism. The newspaper promised lawyer William W. "Plug Hat" Anderson $1,000 if he could spring Packer from his cell. Anderson sought more, allegedly draining Packer's prison account of an additional $1,500.

Bonfils and Tammen were furious, fired Anderson, and refused to pay him his fee. Irate, Anderson called on the two men and harsh—even vile—words were exchanged. "You're not a man at all. You're a low down son of a bitch!" Tammen is said to have shouted during the meeting. Bonfils, seeing Anderson's reaction and afraid he would pull his gun, attacked the lawyer, squeezing him in a headlock and pummeling him with his free hand. Anderson broke free and fired four shots from his .38 revolver. Hit twice, once in the neck, Bonfils was critically wounded, and his partner, also struck by two bullets, was less severely wounded. If not for the intervention of the paper's "sob sister" reporter Polly Pry, who grabbed the pistol from Anderson, both men might have been killed. More luck.

But luck alone did not guide Bonfils's life. He also knew an opportunity to grab a dollar when he saw it. Enter the infamous Teapot Dome scandal of the 1920s.

The Teapot Dome, thirty miles north of Casper, Wyoming, sat atop one of the richest oil fields in the country, just waiting to be tapped. There was one problem: the field was set aside as a naval reserve in case of war. A Denver oilman named Leo Stack and a California petroleum magnate named E. L. Doheny reached an agreement to obtain leases on the Salt Creek field adjacent to the Teapot Dome. The two pools of oil were virtually inseparable.

Albert Fall, the corrupt secretary of the interior in the Warren Harding administration, saw to it that Doheny and another oil baron, Harry Sinclair, received, without competitive bidding, lucrative leases on the Teapot. Fowler wrote that leases were being handed out "like kisses at a wedding." Doheny and Sinclair then reached a deal that cut Stack out of potential millions.

An acquaintance of Bonfils, Stack showed up at the Red Room in 1922 with an interesting tale. He claimed that he owned drilling sites in Wyoming near Teapot Dome and wanted his share of the proceeds. Always ready to launch a crusade against big business, and perhaps seeing a chance to grab some cash, Bonfils agreed to help Stack's cause through the pages of *The Post*. "Mr. Stack claimed they had leased over his head," Bonfils later told a Senate investigative committee. "I entered into a contract with him to help him to enforce his rights. I was to see if we could not get some value for his contract. It was reported to my attorney to be a valid and valuable contract."

On April 16, 1922, the civic-minded Bonfils penned a page-one editorial under the standing headline "So the People May Know." In it, he cast a suspicious eye on the leases, making *The Post* the first newspaper in the country to call the malodorous deal into question. He called the lease a "gift," which, if carried out, "will consummate one of the baldest public-land grabs of the century."

Now on the trail of a sensational story, Bonfils dispatched investigative reporter D. F. Stackelbeck to Fall's Three Rivers Ranch in New Mexico to check into the secretary's sudden wealth. The *Albuquerque Journal* reported that at one point, Fall was nearly bankrupt and failed to pay property taxes for eight years, yet suddenly, he bought additional land for his ranch and was paying off his considerable debt.

Stacklebeck brought back "a shocking and astounding story," including the revelation that it was on Sinclair's private railroad car, parked on a siding at Three Rivers, that Fall and the oil magnate had struck a deal for forty-one leases next to Teapot Dome without a public auction.

Bonfils and *The Post* launched a barrage of editorials savaging Sinclair and the under-the-table lease, an assault that continued unabated until a meeting of all involved in Kansas City. A deal was struck to give Stack $250,000 for his share. In addition, "those interested" (including Bonfils and Tammen) would receive an additional $750,000, to be split this way: 46.5 percent to Stack, 23.25 percent each to Bonfils and Tammen, and 7.5 percent to their lawyer, H. H. Schwartz.

The Post's attacks on Sinclair suddenly ceased. Between September 15 and December 3, 1922, there were no articles mentioning the oil king. There were to be no more editorials, only wire-service stories from subsequent Senate hearings in Washington, DC. Sinclair denied that he'd bought *The Post*'s silence. "I certainly never felt any occasion to buy or attempt to buy the influence of Bonfils's newspaper."

In February 1924, Senators Thomas J. Walsh of Montana and Irvine L. Lenroot of Wisconsin spearheaded a congressional investigation into the Teapot Dome mess. Bonfils showed up voluntarily to testify on his paper's investigation and his financial relationship with Sinclair (some sources said he was alerted that he was to be subpoenaed and simply beat the committee to it).

Bonfils's two appearances before the committee were contentious. He told the senators that there was a conspiracy among Doheny, Sinclair, and Standard Oil–affiliated companies to give Sinclair the Wyoming property, while Doheny got fields in California. The committee was more interested in Bonfils's sudden loss of interest in the oil-scandal story. Lenroot beat on Bonfils about his newspaper's sudden silence until the hot-tempered publisher roared, "You talk to me as though I was a common criminal!"

In The Teapot Dome Scandal, Laton McCartney reprinted the heated exchange between Lenroot and Bonfils, noting that *The Post* co-owner vigorously denied that the attitude of his paper toward Sinclair had anything to do with the contract of settlement:

Lenroot asked Bonfils if "the matter of your attack on Sinclair" was discussed at the conference with Sinclair.

"No, sir," Bonfils replied.

Pressed as to whether the attacks on Sinclair in his paper had not been stopped, Bonfils leaned across the table and said, "They did not cease. They have not ceased. They never shall cease."

Senator Lenroot read a telegram, which said there had been no article on the subject in The Post *from Sept. 15, 1922, to Dec. 3, 1922. The telegram added that there were none during most of 1923 containing any reflection upon Sinclair.*

"We printed the news every day," said Mr. Bonfils.

"Any editorial comments concerning these transactions?"

"I do not think there were."

"Do you mean to testify that there was no change in the attitude of your newspaper concerning these transactions from the beginning?"

"I do."

"You had vigorously attacked Mr. Sinclair and these oil transactions up to a certain time."

"We printed that it was a bad lease and I still think it was."

Wyoming oil leases were given away "like kisses at a wedding"
by corrupt secretary of the interior Albert Fall, who was
convicted on bribery charges and served a year in prison.
Courtesy Library of Congress, LC-H25-22472-D

"You think it was bad, corrupt deal, do you not?"

"We were not blaming Mr. Sinclair for it."

"Is it not a fact that your contract with Mr. Sinclair was not based upon the legal rights of Mr. Stack?"

"That is not true."

"But that this whole deal was for the purpose of purchasing your silence in your newspapers?"

"That is absolutely false."

The Post ballyhooed Bonfils's appearance with an all-caps banner headline on page one, "BONFILS EXPOSES HUGE TEAPOT CONSPIRACY."

The rival *Rocky Mountain News* hooted at Bonfils's version of events:

Apparently devoid of all shame or any sense of morality, Fred G. Bonfils, one of the owners of The Denver Post, *today put on a bold face and coolly confessed to the Senate committee investigating the Teapot Dome oil scandal that he and his partner, H. H. Tammen, as representatives of Leo Stack of Denver, had "shaken down" Harry F. Sinclair for a contract calling for $1 million.*

As Bonfils told his sordid story, senators gasped with astonishment at his admissions and fifty Washington newspapermen, who take pride in the high ethics which govern their acts, hung their heads in shame.

In the end, the US Eighth Circuit Court of Appeals canceled Sinclair's lease on Teapot Dome because of fraud and corruption, which, Bonfils's paper crowed, "was solely due to the efforts of *The Denver Post.*"

In 1927, Fall and Sinclair went on trial in Washington for conspiracy. Among those who testified were Denverites Henry M. Blackmer, whose father (also named Henry) fled to France rather than testify, and A. E. Humphreys Jr. Fall and Sinclair were acquitted. Tried for accepting a $100,000 "loan" from Doheny, Fall was convicted on bribery charges and given a year in prison. Neither Doheny, who died in 1925, nor Sinclair, who died in 1956, ever publicly admitted guilt.

Meanwhile, *The Post* continued on its merry moneymaking ways, shaping politics and financial growth in Denver and driving all of its competitors, except the *News*, out of business. When he died of an ear infection in 1933, Bonfils's estate was worth an estimated $20 million. Though he never seemed to get much joy from it, he reached his goal of gathering enormous wealth.

CHAPTER 9

THE DASHING CLUBMAN

COURTLAND DINES

The sudden appearance of a .25-caliber revolver should have been a warning that the threesome's New Year's Day party in 1924 was coming to an abrupt end, but the *bang!* startled Courtland Dines and his two actress companions.

The incident was a whirlpool of confusion, either as a deliberate attempt to muddy the waters or because Dines and his two friends, silent film stars Mabel Normand and Edna Purviance (pronounced "Pur-VYE-ance"), were in "a hazy condition." Dines had been drinking for two days; he and Purviance, with whom he was linked romantically, were out late on New Year's Eve, and Mabel was nursing a mammoth hangover.

On New Year's afternoon, Edna called her close friend Mabel and told her to come over to Dines's apartment at 325-B North Vermont Avenue in Hollywood. One of the movie industry's legendary party animals, Mabel jumped at the chance. Driven by her chauffeur, she showed up on Dines's doorstep and ordered, "C'mon, you dirty dogs, step into your dance togs and let's go somewheres!"

Dines didn't feel up to it, so Mabel joined the two in a post-holiday get-well celebration in his apartment.

The afternoon wore on. Mabel's chauffeur, Joe Kelly (an alias; his real name was Horace Greer), arrived at Dines's front door to deliver him a Christmas package: a set of brushes and a comb. It was the first of two visits Kelly would make that day. He returned a couple of hours later, determined to take Mabel home because, he said, she was scheduled to have her appendix removed the next day. This wasn't true, although she did have surgery a few days later.

This is where the participants' stories diverge. Kelly, whom police theorized had "a mad, passionate infatuation" for Normand, said that when he entered Dines's apartment the second time, he found Mabel reclining on a divan. He grabbed her by the ankle and told her that he had come to take her home. Dines, according to some accounts, clad only in a silk bathrobe and an undershirt, came out of the kitchen and said she wasn't going anywhere. That's when Kelly fired three shots, one of which penetrated Dines's left lung. It was a matter of self-defense, Kelly said, because Dines reached for a bottle and threatened him with it.

Kelly's version:

I knew that Dines was bigger than myself and before leaving [home] I went to Miss Normand's room and got her revolver. When I stepped into the room I told Miss Normand I had come for her and to get ready. Dines came toward me threateningly.

Dines's version:

All this is tommyrot. All this bunk, this stuff about me reaching for a bottle. I didn't even see the gun when he shot. Edna and I had been to the Ambassador [Hotel] New Year's Eve and we got home late. We were all feeling "low," so low we'd have to use a stepladder to get on a snake's back. And Mabel comes over and she's "low," too. Very low. And we had some drinks too and Mabel gets busy with the mop and broom and scrub rag and the dishcloth. Big-hearted Mabel, always doing something for somebody, and then in walks this moron hophead. He must be a hop, and what's all the shooting for?

Mabel's version:

Joe came in. I noticed nothing unusual about him, and I left the room. I went into Edna's room. I didn't want this chauffeur to see Edna with her dress unhooked so I went and I said to Edna, "Say, you dirty dog, where's your powder puff?" Then, all of a sudden, I heard these terrible things. They sounded like firecrackers. They were popping all over the house.

Courtland Dines

The Denver Post, courtesy of the Western History and Genealogy Department, Denver Public Library

Edna's version:

She claimed, and Kelly's version supported her, that she was in an adjoining bedroom, powdering her face, when bullets flew. She was having an affair with Dines and they either were or weren't engaged, depending on who was doing the telling. Edna told the press, Mr. Dines and I are engaged—and yet we were not engaged. ... He never gave me an engagement ring but there was an understanding between us that we would be married. There was no date.

Dines's family back in Denver, perhaps wearied by his two failed marriages, was not thrilled at the prospect of having Edna in the family. His father, Tyson, vacationing in Gulfport, Mississippi, said, "We would not approve of a marriage to a screen star. We do not consider that the type of womanhood represented in the modern motion picture actress makes good home material."

How all the principals came together is a story in itself.

Dines, who made his fortune as an oilman, popped up in Hollywood in 1923, eager to try his hand as a movie producer. He was little known around town but "lived like a man of large means and [a] free spender." Almost immediately he fell in with Mabel and Edna. Though these were the dark days of Prohibition, all three were fond of booze. They got along famously, said Mabel. "We were just three friends, palling around." On one of their excursions, the trio sailed to Catalina Island off the coast of California, a trip that produced some raucous photographs found in Dines's apartment after the shooting.

This wasn't the first (or last) time that alcohol got the handsome polo player/golfer in hot water. In 1918, he and a friend, Major H. S. Keown of the Canadian-British Recruiting Headquarters, launched a brawl in a Casper, Wyoming, hotel bar after, said a news report, "they imbibed rather freely of various herculean waters and vintages." Some local cowboys made fun of the major's uniform: "Pretty uniform the boy has, eh, wot?" Keown responded, "You're a fine bunch of slackers! Why don't you put on a uniform?" Dines and Keown were pummeled in the ensuing battle.

In 1919, Dines was arrested at midnight for driving recklessly through downtown Denver. In 1927, he was handed a thirty-day sentence

Mabel Normand

Author's collection

Edna Purviance

Author's collection

and fined $50 for driving under the influence of alcohol after he drove off a road in suburban Adams County, and in 1939 he was cited for reckless driving (he fled the scene of a crash but police found him asleep in a nearby hotel) after he ran a red light at West Colfax Avenue and Santa Fe Drive and broadsided another car.

Mabel Normand, a gifted comedic actress and the star of numerous Mack Sennett Keystone Studio films, where she costarred with Charlie Chaplin and Fatty Arbuckle, was one of the screen's biggest names. At the height of her career she was earning $3,000 a week. Slender and petite— she stood only five-foot-one—she had large, dark eyes, which she used to full advantage in her roles as an ingenue. Her quick sense of humor and willingness to risk physical stunts made her a popular costar of the period.

Her movie career flew high from 1910 to 1927, a considerable span in Hollywood years, but it was riddled by alcohol abuse, cocaine addiction, and, in 1922, her involvement in the still-unsolved shooting death of director William Desmond Taylor. Normand, a close friend of Taylor, was the last person other than the killer to see him alive, but police concluded that she had nothing to do with the director's slaying. Nevertheless, it did her career no good.

Hollywood in the 1920s was peppered with scandal and perceived immorality. Comic star Fatty Arbuckle was tried three times (and finally acquitted) for rape in the death of small-time actress Virginia Rappe. The Taylor affair dragged actors and homosexuals through the public prints, and there were the highly publicized drug-related deaths of actors Olive Thomas, Wallace Reid, Barbara La Marr, and Jeanne Eagels. All this bad behavior on the screen and in their private lives brought down the wrath of the federal government on the film industry through the rigid censorship of the Motion Picture Production Code, adopted in 1930.

Normand was as carefree off the screen as she was in her comedic roles for Sennett and Chaplin, both of whom she had affairs with. Born in Staten Island, New York, she worked as a model before landing in films with Chaplin at age sixteen. Ultimately, she would appear in sixty-seven films, many of which she wrote and codirected.

Her friends worried about her health, physical and mental. Defending himself for the New Year's Day shooting, her chauffeur described Mabel as a "poor little girl who couldn't say no when someone suggested a party. She is the sweetest little woman in the world when she is sober but disgusting when otherwise and I hated seeing her going that way.

Courtland Dines decided to take a chance on movie production in 1923 and moved to Hollywood, where he immediately fell in with silent stars Edna Purviance, left, and Mabel Normand, with whom he shared a love of good times and parties.

Courtesy of *The Denver Post*

One of her New Year resolutions was no more wild parties, and the first thing she does is go over to Dines's and start drinking."

When she came out of Edna's bedroom after hearing what she thought were firecrackers, Kelly was gone and Mabel found Dines staggering toward her, covered in blood and clutching his chest. "I've been plugged!" he shouted. Before the police arrived, Mabel and Edna helped Dines into the bedroom and did their best to dress his wound. En route to Good Samaritan Hospital by ambulance, Mabel told him, "Look here, ducky, I don't believe I'll play with you anymore," to which Dines replied, "Nor I with you."

Lying in his hospital bed, surrounded, according to one report, by cigarette smoke and profanity, he said, "I suppose I'll kick the bucket this time. The girls will miss me. We three, Edna, Mabel, and I were just the best pals in the world." Surgeons removed the bullet from Dines's lung and assured all involved that he would survive. The wound was secondary to the fact that he developed pneumonia while hospitalized. It made breathing difficult, and he was in considerable pain. Police warned that if Dines died, the case against the chauffeur would become murder, but his doctor said he was "doing fine." His health improved slowly and he was allowed to go home.

The shooting and the fallout from it damaged the careers of both Mabel Normand and Edna Purviance. For a time, theaters around the country refused to show their films. Mabel's reputation as a party girl and heavy cocaine addict with a $2,000-a-month habit made her unreliable and robbed her of her girlish appearance. She made no movies in 1924 and only four after that until her last, *One Hour Married*, in 1927.

Her wedding in 1926 to suave and mustachioed silent screen star Lew Cody was as unconventional as the rest of her life. He was said to have proposed marriage to her as a joke during a party. She accepted in the same spirit and they were married in a quickie ceremony by a Ventura County judge in California. They never lived together but remained married until her death in 1930. In 1928, she made a train trip to visit him in Denver, where he was appearing in a stage play. There is no record that she called on her playmate "Court" while in town.

Mabel's health, plagued for years by repeated bouts with tuberculosis, finally gave out on February 23, 1930, in a sanitarium in Monrovia, California. She was thirty-seven years old. Cody, fifty years old, died in his sleep of heart disease in 1934.

An accomplished polo player and golfer, Courtland Dines
was the very image of a man-about-town clubman.
His active social life led to four marriages.

The Denver Post, courtesy of the Western History and Genealogy Department, Denver Public Library

The career of Edna Purviance, twenty-eight, fared no better. Discovered by Chaplin at an open call for "the prettiest girl in California" when she was nineteen, she was soon his leading lady on and off the screen. Like Mabel, she was short, only five-foot-two, and blessed with a sweet, girlish countenance and expressive eyes. She starred in thirty films over eight years for Chaplin, but as the years passed, her baby-faced beauty and slim figure faded. In *Chaplin: His Life and Art*, David Robinson wrote, "It soon became evident that Edna was not to be Chaplin's leading lady. Even before *A Woman of Paris* (1923) Chaplin had observed that she had grown too 'matronly' for comedy roles. Her drinking made her weight unpredictable and her acting unreliable." Her confidence shaken, Edna grew "unbelievably timid and unable to act in even the simplest scene without some great difficulty." Chaplin, a prodigious womanizer (he once claimed to have had sex with more than two thousand women), threw Edna over for much younger partners, some barely sixteen years old.

Kelly's trial for shooting Dines was a sterling example of obfuscation. Normand, Purviance, and Dines all testified that the details were "a little hazy." Dines was out of town early in the trial, in Denver at his ailing father's beside, but when he did show up to testify, he said he couldn't even remember that Kelly had shot him. All three denied that they were drunk, but Mabel told jurors, "Dines was not exactly drunk but he had plenty."

Mabel was forever the actress on the stand. A reporter for the *Los Angeles Herald* observed:

> *Miss Normand [had] a broad—oh, very broad—"a." It is "a" in "bawth," "cawn't," "rawther," and "pawdon." So like dear old Lonnon!*
>
> *Miss Normand's conversational hands ... fairly chatter. They are voluble, loquacious. [She] illustrated every answer with a gesture. Her hands point out that delicate distinction between a man who is drunk and a man who is only "drinking." She impersonates the pouring of the drink. She illustrates the exact size of a right and proper drink, the amount remaining is measured by her hands, and the fluttering fingers go through the "business" of the convivial scene.*
>
> *Her hands show the jury just how the door opened into the bedroom, just how she powdered her nose, just the way she gathered up the offending cigarette butts which marred the order of Dines's apartment on her arrival.*

Kelly declined to testify because, he said, he would "rather go to the penitentiary than say anything that would hurt Miss Normand."

After Kelly's trial for assault with intent to commit murder—a jury acquitted him after only four hours, in large part because Dines testified that he didn't know if it was Kelly who had shot him—a wire-service reporter wrote:

> *In another day it would have been Mabel Normand whose name was on every tongue. But that day is past. Mabel is a madcap; everybody knows her, everybody is her friend; her secrets are everybody's knowledge. But Edna is different. Edna is, in effect, a recluse. She doesn't mix much. When you come right down to cases, there are not half a dozen people in Hollywood who know Edna as intimate friends know each other.*

Even after Edna's last film appearance in 1927, Chaplin kept her on the payroll for years. She drifted into retirement and obscurity, married an airline pilot in 1938, and died of throat cancer in Los Angeles on January 11, 1958, at age sixty-two.

After the scandal and his brush with death in Hollywood, Dines, thirty-four, resumed his life as an athletic, mustachioed, and well-to-do Denver oilman and society figure who enjoyed his leisure time, sometimes too much. He was once referred to in print as "a dashing clubman and sportsman with a flair for profitable enterprises." Born into an old-line Denver family in 1889, Dines received an elite education. After elementary school at Emerson School in Denver, he went to Holbrook's Military Academy in Ossining, New York; Phillips Exeter Academy in Andover, Massachusetts; and earned a degree from Yale University.

Yet despite his education and success at business, the dashing clubman was a bust at marriage. Wed four times, three of his wives divorced him on grounds of extreme cruelty, one adding "inebriety" to the charges. When his first wife, Doris Leonora Carnahan, the 1917 women's state golfing champion and granddaughter of early Colorado mining man and banker Eben Smith, asked for a divorce, he didn't protest. "The trouble is largely my own fault. I have a rotten temper that no woman could very well live with. This caused perpetual incompatibility."

His marital luck didn't get any better. His second wife, Eleanor (Mrs. Harry P.) Harley, a Massachusetts widow described as "beautiful, charming, and talented," visited Denver frequently before their marriage. However, she split from him in 1923, barely four years after they wed.

He married wife number three, the "exceedingly attractive" Helen Gibson, at her mother's home in Congress Park in 1925, but they divorced five years later.

By February 1931, Dines found himself recovering from ongoing kidney problems—probably due, in part, to his drinking—at the Taggert Ranch, five miles from Tabernash in the Colorado Rockies. There, according to newspaper reports, he was struck by a convulsion that caused him to stumble down a flight of stairs and sustain a fractured and dislocated left shoulder. Still traveling in style, Dines was transported through a snowstorm down to Denver on the private railroad car of William Freeman, president of the Moffat Road.

He finally got the marriage thing right in 1935 when he married Betty Arbon, a wealthy New York widow, after a long friendship. They stayed married until his death.

The clubman who incorrectly predicted his death after the 1924 affray, suffered a heart attack at his home at 492 South Marion Street in 1944 and succumbed to another attack at St. Joseph Hospital on March 13, 1945.

CHAPTER 10

THE GANGSTER WHO LOVED COLORADO

"DIAMOND JACK" ALTERIE

In Chicago, he was Louis "Two Gun" Alterie, a beady-eyed hit man with slicked-back hair outfitted in sartorial splendor complete with spats and a gardenia boutonniere. In Colorado, he was "Diamond Jack" Alterie, a Tom Mix-style cowboy who wrestled steers and couldn't stay out of trouble with the law.

He was born Leland Varain in 1886 on a ranch in northern California, where he learned to rope and ride—skills that would endear him to Colorado audiences in the 1920s.

Alterie was sturdily built. He stood almost six feet tall and weighed more than two hundred pounds with an outsized chest and arms. Acquaintances described him as "swarthy." And he was tough. As Louis Alterie (a name he adopted after a boxer friend of his by the same name died), he was an enforcer for the Dean O'Banion mob in Chicago, with several gang rivals' deaths attributed to him. When O'Banion was gunned down by opposing mobsters in his flower shop in 1924, Alterie, O'Banion's right-hand man, challenged the shooters to meet him at State and Madison Streets, Chicago's busiest intersection, to shoot it out with him and his ever-present pair of .45s. No one took him up on it.

"Diamond Jack" Alterie, also known as Louis Alterie and Leland Varain, worked as a dapper hit man for bootlegger Dean O'Banion during Chicago's gang wars. When O'Banion was shot to death in his flower shop in 1924, Alterie "retired" to his four-thousand-acre ranch in Jarre Canyon near Sedalia, Colorado.

Author's collection

With the bootlegging war claiming his fellow mobsters—forty-five were killed in five years—Alterie decided it was time to get out of town for a vacation. He chose Colorado, which meshed nicely with his memories of wide-open western spaces and his love of ranch life. In 1924, he bought 4,000 acres of land in Jarre Canyon, nestled in the hills on Highway 67, six miles south of Sedalia and twenty-five miles south of Denver. He entertained his Chicago cronies at his Diamond V Ranch, including O'Banion before his death, and Frank Gusenberg (who, in 1929, miraculously survived for three hours after the Saint Valentine's Day Massacre in a Chicago garage before dying of nine bullet wounds in a hospital—without ever naming those who shot him).

Alterie's first of many run-ins with Colorado law enforcement took place in January 1925, when Chicago police issued warrants (later withdrawn) for his and Gusenberg's arrest for a robbery. Douglas County sheriff Roy McKissack, an old-school country lawman, chased them down. "I'll get 'em or run 'em both out of the country," he bragged. He did arrest them, but it was a cordial collaring. At a dinner in the sheriff's honor, Alterie presented McKissack with a gold sheriff's badge studded with diamonds because, Jack said, "He came up there after me alone. When I gave up, I shook hands with a 'real' police officer."

As he grew more comfortable with his Colorado lifestyle, Diamond Jack sold his Jarre Canyon property and leased a 3,000-acre spread on Sweetwater Lake in northwestern Colorado. He called it the Diamond J and operated it as a dude ranch. Known today as the Sweetwater Ranch Resort, it still caters to would-be cowpokes.

He loved to dress western and play the drugstore cowboy. He favored a red satin shirt, handmade inlaid boots, silver spurs, and tan pants, all topped by an enormous beige ten-gallon hat of the style made famous by movie cowboy Tom Mix. But what he liked most were diamonds—on his cuffs, on his fingers and, especially, on the large belt buckle it was said he won for steer wrestling. He was truly "Diamond Jack."

Diamond Jack strutted his stuff, motoring around Colorado in a long beige Lincoln convertible with a huge set of horns mounted on the radiator. He was in his element in 1925 when he threw a three-day rodeo at the Stockyards Stadium featuring noted female competitors, including

"Diamond Jack" Alterie sported an enormous
ten-gallon cowboy hat when he relocated to Colorado.
His nickname came from his love of the precious stones—
on his cuffs, fingers, and on a large belt buckle.
Courtesy of the Western History and Genealogy Department, Denver Public Library, X-22166

Ione Snodgrass, Rose Smith, and Mae Louise Martin, "the only child trick rider ... in roundup events." *The Denver Post*, which loved such public displays, threw a street party in front of its Champa Street offices to publicize the event. Bombs exploded, there was music by Ernie Moore and His Jazzerinos, dancing by Red Sublett and his trick mule, and, as a grand finale, airplanes buzzing overhead to drop parachutes carrying free tickets to the rodeo.

The rodeo was a huge success. At each performance, Diamond Jack galloped into the arena astride his stallion, "King George," splendorous in his dazzling cowboy outfit, which included furry white chaps. He was hailed by entrants as "King of Roundup Producers" and became a rodeo participant on the last day of the event by bulldogging a Brahma bull. He put on the rodeo again in 1926, publicizing it by tooling around town in his Lincoln with three Native American chiefs in full headdress and a large banner proclaiming, "Rocky Mountain Roundup/Stockyard Stadium Aug. 5–7–8/The Flaming Frontier American—Now" on its side. An added attraction was John Aasen, hailed as the world's tallest man at eight-feet-nine and a half inches.

Jack not only changed his lifestyle when he moved to Colorado, but also acquired a new wife. In February 1927, at age forty-one, he divorced his first wife, Mabel, and almost immediately wed eighteen-year-old Ermina (Erma) Rossi, the daughter of Denver mobster Mike Rossi, who was serving a life sentence at Cañon City for shooting and killing his wife, Caroline, in their attorney's office while arguing over a divorce settlement. Mike Rossi congratulated the newlyweds from his cell: "God bless Ermina and Diamond Jack. They will be very happy." Mabel's family was happy too. "We're glad to get rid of him," said one.

A new wife didn't keep Diamond Jack out of trouble. He couldn't completely shake his life as a hit man for the mob; Jack was proud of his guns and knew how to use them. In a 1955 reminiscence written for the *Denver Posse Brand Book*, John Johnson Lipsey recalled with wonder his visit to the Diamond J when Alterie invited him to one of the ranch's outbuildings:

> *On the shelves was the damnedest collection of modern firearms I have ever seen. There were shotguns (double- and single-barreled, pump and automatic), rifles (single-shot, pump and automatic—in many makes, most models, most calibers, plus many army*

pieces—U.S. and foreign), a combination shotgun and rifle, pistols (many calibers, some for target shooting, some for business; revolvers and automatics); and machine guns and submachine guns—"Tommy guns." There was not an antique or a museum piece in the arsenal, which, I guess, totaled some 250 pieces. Every piece seemed to have been recently cleaned, oiled and wiped. No rust, no dust.

As further insurance against intruders bent on ending Jack's life, machine-gun nests flanked the entrance to the ranch.

Gunplay seemed to follow Jack. In 1927, he was gunned down at close range in an argument over the sale of some horses on his Diamond J ranch. The shooter: his older brother, Bert Varain. The brothers were at the breakfast table when their quarrel heated up. Jack pushed Bert, who left the room and was back minutes later with hate in his eyes and a shotgun in his hands. Jack saw him at the last minute and threw up his hand to ward off the blast, which tore a gaping hole in his upper left arm and shoulder. Erma, his wife of six months, rushed him to the hospital in Glenwood Springs, probably saving his life. "She's got nerve, that gal," Alterie said later. Doctors removed 146 pellets of No. 4 birdshot, but Jack was in a forgiving mood and refused to press charges. "Oh, I could not kill him or prosecute him. He was my brother."

Two years later, Jack tried his hand at mining promotion in Leadville, Colorado, when he organized the Diamond Jack Mining Company, whose president was Leland A. Varain (Alterie's real name). It was incorporated with 500,000 shares at one dollar per. Brochures were mailed out with the invitation to mail checks to the Carbonate American National Bank in Leadville. In them, promises were made that $100,000 would be spent to bore 400-foot shaft on a 150-acre site. It never came to pass because Jack's quick temper got the best of him again. He was run out of town by local authorities, who grabbed him after an attempted assault on the owner of local candy store.

Diamond Jack's love of firearms and his frequent drunken brawls led to his expulsion from his Colorado paradise in 1932. He enjoyed a relatively clean life out West unless he was on one of his legendary drinking binges, one of which unfolded when he traveled in November to Glenwood Springs, thirty-seven miles from his ranch on Sweetwater Lake.

He got drunk and challenged another man to a fight in the Denver Hotel just behind the train station in Glenwood. Unfortunately, the

Jack Alterie frequently entertained friends and family at
his Diamond V Ranch south of Sedalia, Colorado.
His one-time Chicago mob boss, Dean O'Banion, stands
at left in the front row with his wife, Viola, on his left.
Alterie is in the middle, with his arms folded, and his wife, Ermina,
with a feather in her hair, is on the left in the back row.
Courtesy of the Castle Rock, Colorado, Museum

Ever the showman, Jack Alterie motored around Denver
in his Lincoln convertible loaded down with Native Americans
in headdresses and banners to publicize his upcoming
Rocky Mountain Roundup rodeo in August 1926.

The Denver Post, courtesy of the Western History and Genealogy Department, Denver Public Library

man he chose was Whitey Hutton, a burly mechanic for the Rio Grande Railroad and a former boxer. Hutton left Alterie bruised and bleeding. Outraged, Jack left the hotel and returned with a shotgun, but was disarmed in the lobby by a hotel porter. Still in a drunken rage, he went to his room, retrieved two .45 automatics, and went hunting for Hutton.

He mistakenly believed that Hutton had taken refuge in a room occupied by traveling salesmen Marc Waynick and George Barr, and he fired blindly through their door. One of his shots grazed Barr's leg and burrowed through Waynick's thigh. Waynick died the following summer, but, luckily for Alterie, not from the bullet wound but from a lung tumor. Instead of a murder charge, Alterie went on trial for assault with intent to kill, and Judge John T. Shumate fined him $1,250 and gave him two options: spend five years in the state penitentiary or find another place to live for five years. Alterie chose Chicago, although he was frequently reported to be in Cheyenne, Wyoming, and may have slipped back into Colorado from time to time.

His life was about to come full circle. Exiting Eastwood Towers on Chicago's North Side with his wife on the morning of July 18, 1935, Alterie was peppered in the head and neck by shotgun pellets fired by hired killers lying in wait in a first-story apartment across the street. He was dead almost as soon as he hit the sidewalk. His wife, her candy-striped pink-and-white dress spattered with his blood, tried to reassure him that help was on the way, but he knew better: "It's all right, honey. They cannot help me now." A more romantic version of his farewell had him saying, "I can't help it, Bambina, but I'm going."

In a wild touch of irony, Alterie's life was ended by the very "rental ambush" he had invented years before to get rid of rivals. He never had a chance to use those two guns he was famous for. He once told a reporter, "In Chicago, they'll never take my guns away. They can't prevent me from carrying the two rods there. I need them to protect my life. I'm not saying that I can't be killed, because I can."

He was known to carry up to $30,000 in cash, but when police went through his pockets they found only $23.40, a rosary, and a note from a woman asking for a loan of $3 to help her injured sister.

CHAPTER 11

THE IRON LADY
PEARL O'LOUGHLIN

The little girl's body lay on the bottom of the lake, not ten feet from shore, her legs doubled under her, her arms bent upward at the elbows, her hands clasped across her chest.

That was where ten-year-old Leona O'Loughlin, called by some "the sweetest and most obedient child," finished her young life. How she got there remains a matter of conjecture and controversy.

October 14, 1930, was one of those unusually warm fall evenings in Denver. Pearl O'Loughlin, as she always did, tucked the children in their beds—her stepdaughter, Leona, in one room, and her son, Douglas Millican, in another—at about eight o'clock. Pearl's husband, Leo, a detective with the Denver Police Department, worked nights. As she often did, she drove the mile or so to police headquarters in downtown to pick him up when his shift ended near midnight.

The next morning, Leona was nowhere to be found. Her bed was empty. Her school chums, including her close friend Betty Scott, who lived across the way on Tremont Place, hadn't seen her, and they walked the four blocks to Cathedral School without her. Pearl canvassed the neighbors, hoping they had spotted Leona that morning. Leo, who knew his daughter's routine very well, worried that she hadn't had breakfast and that she'd left without even a "good morning." He called the school; no luck. He hurried to police headquarters to report her missing. His detective partner, Clarence Jones, tried to reassure him, but O'Loughlin insisted that a missing-person alarm be spread.

Little Leona O'Loughlin's body was found in shallow water
at the edge of Berkeley Park Lake after a frantic search.
The murdered girl was ten years old.

Rocky Mountain News, courtesy of the Western History and Genealogy Department, Denver Public Library

Rallying around their distressed colleague, police mobilized, scouring the city and sending out a description of the missing girl, described as blond, blue eyed, and big for her age at about eighty pounds. Denver police leaped into action and so did investigators from the district attorney's office, the Colorado State Patrol, county sheriffs, and federal officers. The police floated various scenarios—that "a fiend" (meaning a child molester) might have abducted her, that one of the criminals O'Loughlin had arrested was exacting revenge, or that Leona had had a disagreement with her parents and simply ran away.

But on the morning of October 17, a North Denver grocer taking an afternoon stroll through Berkeley Park spied a girl's body lying in shallow water a few feet from the edge of the lake. It was quickly determined that the submerged form was that of the missing ten-year-old.

That afternoon, police pulled in Pearl O'Loughlin, Leona's thirty-two-year-old stepmother, for questioning; she was their prime suspect from the beginning. The interrogation went on for an hour as Clark asked her point blank, "Why did you put the child in the lake?" "Who took her from the house?" "Who helped you?" Pearl adamantly and repeatedly denied his accusations.

Two days later, police arrested her, charging her with murdering little Leona. In a new twist, however, they accused her of poisoning the girl by putting powdered glass in her dinner the night she vanished; an autopsy found a teaspoon of the substance in her stomach. Pearl readily admitted she made a dinner of lamb chops, beans, rice, and pineapple for the family that night, but denied adding any glass. Nevertheless, her husband, suffering extreme stomach pains and a high fever, was admitted to Saint Joseph Hospital where it was discovered that he, too, had glass in his digestive system. Neither Pearl nor her son was taken ill. Leo's father, Dennis, later told police that he found glass in his sugar bowl some weeks earlier.

Nine days after her body was retrieved from the lake, little Leona O'Loughlin was buried with a requiem mass at Immaculate Conception Cathedral on East Colfax Avenue. More than 2,000 onlookers, including dozens of her schoolmates, crowded the cathedral and the streets outside. Six little boys dressed in dark-blue suits carried the small white casket down the center aisle to the doors of the cathedral; six little girls dressed in white followed. Her body was taken to Fort Collins, sixty-eight miles away, and buried in the family plot at Grandview Cem-

The *Rocky Mountain News* devoted its entire front page
of October 20, 1930, to Pearl O'Louglin's arrest. The claim
that her stepdaughter was "poisoned" turned out to be untrue.

Rocky Mountain News, courtesy of the Western History and Genealogy Department, Denver Public Library

etery next to her mother, who died in 1928. Pearl did not attend the funeral.

The city was shocked. Could a young mother actually murder her own stepchild and coldly dispose of her body in a lake? Photographs of a grim-faced Pearl in the newspapers gave no hint.

Pearl Esta Weisz Millican O'Loughlin was born in Denver on July 12, 1898, one of four children of Arthur and Lillie Weisz. She took a path many young women of the era followed. An outstanding student, she graduated from West High School in 1916 and went to Barnes Business College, planning to be a stenographer. There she met fellow student John Millican, known as "Billy," and married him in Boulder on February 4, 1920. She and Millican had a son, Douglas, in 1922, and she divorced the boy's father in October 1928. Three months later, in January 1929, she married Leo O'Loughlin, the result, friends said, of a warm friendship that ripened into love.

She was tall, five-foot-nine, and slender, with "a figure more angular and muscular than curved in its contours," said *The Denver Post*. "The kind of woman who can always be counted on to look after herself." Blue-gray, almost sad eyes overshadowed her slightly protruding front teeth. Some thought her attractive.

The O'Loughlin household was not a happy one. Only two months after their marriage in Golden, Pearl and Leo, both previously married and divorced, began bickering, usually about money. She spent it; Leo didn't like that. His wife did all the work—washing, cooking, sweeping, and marketing. "Yes, she did all the marketing because I gave her all the money I made," he groused.

He told a reporter that Pearl once asked him to scold Leona for being untidy and tearing her clothes. He told her to look after her own kid, and, after that, "Pearl never complained again." Besides, he said, she nagged him with her "insatiable desire" for money, which she often spent on her relatives. She countered that she hadn't had a new dress "or money enough to buy one" for more than two years.

During her November 1930 trial, Pearl complained to *The Post's* renowned feature writer Frances "Pinky" Wayne, "The curse of the O'Loughlin family is their ungovernable temper. It is Leo's only fault, but it consumes all his virtues. I gave up my career [as a dance teacher] to become a homemaker, to look after his little girl and my little boy and to make a good wife. It would take a block of marble to fill that last order."

Pearl O'Loughlin as a young woman
Courtesy of the Dianne Millican Miller Collection

She was miserable. "There wasn't a peaceful minute. I was so unhappy at that time that nothing really mattered." She once threatened to drown Douglas in the bathtub and kill herself.

There was the difficulty of merging two families, his ten-year-old daughter and her eight-year-old son. Pearl was working on becoming a Christian Scientist but deferred to Leo and joined the Catholic Church, and Leona and a set of stillborn twins born to the couple were baptized in the church.

The couple separated four times—Pearl once fled with the household's furniture—and even filed divorce suits on each other in May 1930, each claiming "cruelty." They withdrew suits in July because, they agreed, Leona needed a mother.

Leo's brother, Frank, suffering his own marital problems, moved into the O'Loughlins' two-story Denver square (now demolished) at 2320 Tremont Place, a stone's throw from Ebert School, in mid-1930. His presence did not improve matters.

Pearl and Frank were openly hostile to each other. "I had no use for Frank O'Loughlin from the moment I knew what he had done to his family," she said, "and after I heard he was talking viciously about little Leona I determined to face him with his lies as I had with his unfaithfulness to his little crimes." What he had done, she said, was abandon his family in California to move to Denver. He denied it. He, in turn, criticized Leona's behavior and once threatened to have her sent to reform school if she didn't stop making so much noise. That made Pearl even angrier. "This is our home and if Frank does not like the way I am running my home he can move."

The simmering feud came to a head when a mysterious fire broke out in his clothes closet. "My clothing was burned," he said. "Others in the house assigned the fire to spontaneous combustion but I felt it wasn't. There was a family quarrel over the matter and it came down largely to myself and Mrs. O'Loughlin. After the quarrel we didn't speak, and haven't since. Naturally, under those circumstances I ate my meals elsewhere."

After her arrest, a tag team of police officers grilled Pearl closely for two hours on Sunday morning, afternoon, and night; from 9:50 p.m. to 4:20 a.m. the following Wednesday, and from 9 p.m. to 2 a.m. on Thursday. She managed little sleep and during her first two days in jail was given no food, only a glass of orange juice, which she sipped until she discovered a cockroach floating in it. She wasn't allowed to bathe until Thursday. At one point, Pearl said to police captain Albert Clark, one of those questioning her, "Tell me, Captain, how long is this going to go on?" To which Clark smiled and said, "I can't say, Mrs. O'Loughlin. I believe I can hold out as long as you can."

She repeatedly told her questioners, "I didn't do it! I didn't do it! Don't you know I didn't do it?"

Finally, after thirty-six hours of intense police interrogation, Chief Robert Reed announced to the press that he had extracted a confession from her, saying that she told them, "I did it—I alone am to blame—take me out and hang me." He said, "We've nearly completed the major investigation of the murder and every important fact points to Mrs. O'Loughlin as the perpetrator of the crime." But there was no written statement and the final session was interrupted when her lawyer, John Keating, showed up with a writ of *habeas corpus*, claiming unlawful imprisonment and that she was held incommunicado.

Her trial began on Friday, November 28, 1930. Judge Henley Calvert, trying to prevent the proceedings from turning into a vaudeville show, allowed only witnesses, prospective jurors, court employees, newspaper reporters, and attorneys into the courtroom until a jury was selected.

Pearl strode into court on the first day carefully dressed in a close-fitting black felt hat "and a pout on her reddened lips," said a *Post* reporter. The paper's Wayne was more precise:

> *She wore black satin made in long straight lines with a wide white lace collar and a string of amber beads just the color of the [tufts] of reddish hair beneath the close-fitting black felt hat with its turned-up rim. She looked positively girlish as she removed her top coat, folded it, placed it on the table by her side and leaned her head upon it as though she had suddenly become ill or faint and needed support.*
>
> *In the front row of spectators sat her husband, staring at her with hatred in his dark eyes. She stared back, subtly turning her hands to show him that she was no longer wearing his wedding ring. Why? "The day will come when Leo will ask me to put it back."*

The testimony about the condition of Leona's body was particularly graphic. Under questioning by prosecutors, Dr. W. S. Dennis, the city's pathologist, testified that her left arm was out of her sweater. Her arms

Leo O'Loughlin

Rocky Mountain News, courtesy of the Western History and Genealogy Department, Denver Public Library

Pearl O'Loughlin and her son by her first marriage,
Douglas Millican, shared a home with Leo O'Loughlin
and his daughter, Leona. It was an unhappy household.

Courtesy of the Dianne Millican Miller Collection

and legs were flexed and her mouth and tongue protruded. The outfit she was wearing when her body was discovered was pulled from a blue laundry bag and shown to the court and a teary-eyed Pearl.

His clinical description of the head wounds was even more wrenching for Pearl, who broke down in tears at several revelations:

> *On top of the head was a small ragged wound, one-half inch in length that penetrated the scalp but did not reach the bone.*
>
> *On the left side there was a wound about an inch long. This split the scalp but did not reach the bone. There was no blood on the body. There was no evidence of criminal assault or such mistreatment. After the scalp was turned back there were several bruises. Opening the head, no fracture or gross hemorrhage was noted.*
>
> *QUESTION—From your autopsy what, in your opinion, was the cause of death?*
> *ANSWER—From the findings the cause of death was a combination of concussion and asphyxiation.*

His conclusion: She was alive when she was dumped in the lake and died of drowning.

Pearl already had been taken to view Leona's body at the Horan Mortuary, another attempt by police to break her down. She testified:

> *Her little body was lying there with a gold cover on it. They were standing around. They kept me six feet away from her. While I was looking at her poor little face all her clothing was brought in. I was asked if this belonged to her and if this belonged to her until all had been shown. Before that Mr. [District Attorney Earl] Wettengel said, "Did you throw that baby in the lake?" I said, "How could I do such a thing, throw that baby in a lake?"*

In recounting the moment, an anguished Pearl told the court, "[Her hair] was pushed back, there was mud in it. They hadn't washed her face. There were streaks on her little nose." Officers accompanying her allowed her to kneel beside the coffin and pray.

The evidence against her was overwhelmingly circumstantial. The district attorney's office found a tire iron with traces of blood and hair on it in the trunk of the family Chrysler but never tested it to see if the blood belonged to Leona; Dr. Dennis said he couldn't. Few medical practitioners were trained in forensic toxicology at the time; only New York City had a dedicated toxicology laboratory, established in 1915. Using DNA for genetic fingerprinting would not be developed for another fifty-four years. Pearl's fingerprints were not found on the tool and the "hair" turned out to be a fragment of dyed fiber. Investigators also found traces of sand, which, they said, matched that at Berkeley Park, in the family washing machine. Pearl told investigators that a blood-soaked rag found stuffed under the backseat cushion of the auto was the result of stopping a nosebleed her son had suffered. Tests were able to conclude that it was human blood but nothing more.

The prosecution clung to its theory that Pearl tried to kill Leona and Leo with a dose of powdered glass in their food, but city toxicologist Dr. Frances McConnell testified that while such a "poison" could make a person ill it would not kill them. "A myth," she called it.

There were repeated arguments on what, exactly, ground glass was and how it might have gotten into the family's food. Her attorneys said it was an ingredient found in common household cleansers, available to anyone at any hardware store.

The jury was not allowed to hear her confession to Clark because, Judge Calvert said, police used "undue force" to solicit it. "I certainly don't think confessions obtained under these circumstances are proper and they will not be admitted in this case." A critical point in the prosecution's case collapsed.

The major flaw in Pearl's defense was her unexplained whereabouts the night Leona disappeared from her home. From the first day she was questioned by police, she refused to say where she was. At first, she told a story that she was visiting her hairdresser/friend, Ethel Sparr, but Sparr, her conscience bothering her, went to the police and contradicted Pearl's story. Pearl, she said, did briefly stop by her house near Berkeley Park, but "she begged me to establish an alibi in case anyone wanted to know where she was that night."

Still, Pearl never wavered in her steadfast stance that she did not take Leona's life. An enthralled public, following the case in the daily papers, dubbed her "The Iron Lady" for her persistence.

After the all-male jury deliberated for four hours (with time out for dinner), Pearl was found guilty of murder on December 8, 1930, and sentenced to life at the Colorado State Penitentiary in Cañon City. When the verdict was read, she sat upright in her chair, her fingers interlocked, but revealed no emotion. Her husband, on the other hand, couldn't hide his approval. "The jury's right," he later told *The Post*. "She's guilty and she's got it coming to her. I'm satisfied." He also alluded to the attitude of his police department colleagues: "I picked her as the guilty party at the very first. The very moment I learned what had happened to Leona, I suspected my wife. She killed Leona to get my property."

Pearl and Leo finally got the divorce they had so often threatened in June 1931 while Pearl was still in Denver County Jail, pending appeals. On April 20, 1932, she was taken by automobile, in the company of three deputy sheriffs, to Cañon City to begin her sentence. Her outfit, a faded brown dress, black coat, and green hat, was decidedly less fashionable than what she wore to court. "Please write to me," she said to the few friends who gathered to see her off.

Ray Humphreys, a former newspaperman and the district attorney's lead investigator, wrote an account of the case in a 1946 book, *Denver Murders*. He praised Leo O'Loughlin, who was allowed to take part in the investigation, as "one of the ace sleuths of the Denver police department," but even Humphreys couldn't say with confidence that the police proved their case against Pearl. It was, he wrote, "'an example of circumstantial evidence of the purest ray serene,' as the poets might say." He couldn't pinpoint a motive and admitted that Pearl's inquisitors never elicited a genuine confession from her. His conclusion: "The district attorney, the police, and the public have yet to find out why Leona was slain, just how, just where, and just when."

After almost twenty years of silence about Leona's death and repeated denials of her role in it, Pearl "told all" in a 1950 prison interview with *Rocky Mountain News* managing editor Robert Chase, Warden Roy Best, her brother John Weisz, and her lawyer, John Shireman. Her scenario, dismissed by skeptical politicians and prison officials, was improbable.

The story revolved around an accidental overdose of the powerful sedative Allonal, which Leo took to help him sleep because his marriage was in turmoil.

> *I had put Douglas to bed. Leona had gone in to undress herself so it must have been about 8 o'clock. Then Leona came downstairs. She was acting silly. I could see that something was the matter.*

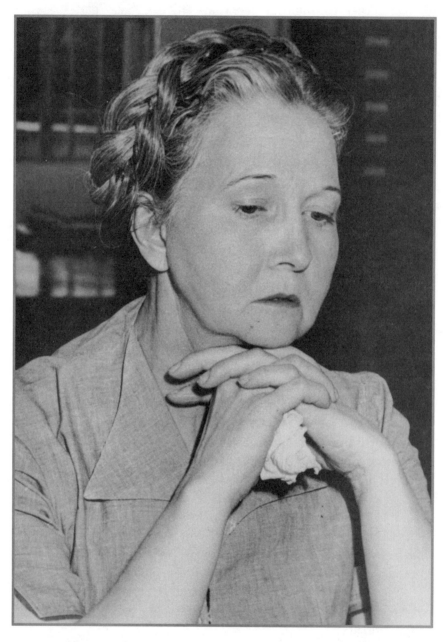

Pearl O'Loughlin was fifty-three years old when she was released
from the state penitentiary in Cañon City in 1951, having served
nineteen years for her stepdaughter Leona's murder.

Rocky Mountain News, courtesy of the Western History and Genealogy Department, Denver Public Library

"Mother, I took those pills."

I thought, "He'll kill me." I was scared to death of him. The children were scared of him. The only time I dared defy him was when he picked on the children. A woman will do that for a child. My first thought was that I must get help, that I must get to [her brother] John.

I got her in the car and we started for John's house. I kept talking to her and slapping her, trying to keep her awake. If I had known then what I know now, I could have done differently. But you don't know what you'll do until you do it. I hardly knew what I was doing or where we were going. I was trying only to get help.

Until you are scared, you don't know what you'll do when you are scared. I knew what he would do to me. I thought I would have to get rid of her. I thought they'd think somebody took her if I did that. I drove over by Berkeley Lake. She was a big girl—we had to get 14-year-old size clothes for her—she was big, full through the chest. I couldn't lift her out of the car. I dragged her. I didn't drag her very far into the water—I don't really know how far.

I didn't look around. I couldn't think. I didn't hardly know what I was doing. I only thought I must get her where Leo wouldn't find her. I didn't want my family brought into it. I kept thinking that if they didn't find her, there wouldn't be anything done and that if they did I wouldn't talk.

Chase believed her. So did Warden Best, who campaigned vigorously for her release. So did Governor Walter Johnson, who signed an executive order that led to her parole. The imaginative version, revealed nineteen years after Pearl went to prison, overlooked the abrasions on Leona's head, the fact that she was alive when she was dragged into the lake, the powdered glass found in her stomach, and the blood-spattered tire iron.

She didn't clear up why she refused, from day one, to say where she was during those crucial three hours the night Leona vanished. But there is an obvious clue in a 1932 appeal of her conviction to the Colorado Supreme Court, in which she said she was out with a man. "She said to Leo, 'You don't believe I was out with a man, do you?' And Leo says, 'I do not.' 'Well,' she said, 'I was.' 'Well,' says Leo, 'name him.' She says, 'If I name him,' she says, 'you will go out and get him.'"

Backed by the publication of her version of Leona's death, Pearl O'Loughlin walked out of the penitentiary a free woman at ten minutes past midnight on June 30, 1951, having served nineteen years and three months. She was fifty-three years old and her red hair was decidedly going to gray. Her first response to her release: "I'm speechless."

The state gave her the same going-away gift all ex-prisoners received—$25 and a set of civilian clothes—and she immediately went to Warden Best's home next to the prison, where she had worked for him during her prison term, to resume taking care of his stepdaughter, Suzanne. It wasn't allowed. Under state statutes, a parolee was required to leave Fremont County, but she moved in with the family on Best's ranch just over the line in neighboring El Paso County, where she lived until Best died in 1954.

Pearl refused an offer to work as a nurse at Spears Chiropractic Sanitarium in Denver, a city she had no desire to return to, choosing instead to move to California where she resumed, not her maiden name Weisz, but that of her first husband, John Millican, without explanation. She died following a stroke at age eighty-eight in San Diego on January 15, 1987. Family members say she never spoke of the murder.

CHAPTER 12

THE PERFECT SALESMAN

FRED WARD

In the early 1950s, Fred Ward was the largest Hudson car dealer in the West.

That doesn't mean much to the generations that followed after the car company disappeared in 1954, but for thirty years it was a very big deal. The slow decline of the Hudson brand—which reached its sales zenith in 1929 with 300,000 sold, behind only Ford and Chevrolet—helped lead to the spectacular downfall of one of the company's best salesmen.

The hard-charging and affable Ward's empire was exposed as a mirage in the summer of 1951 after he was accused of obtaining bank loans under false pretenses, selling cars he didn't own, and bouncing checks to friends and investors. Ultimately, it would lead to a term at the Colorado State Penitentiary.

As his financial world was crashing down around him, Ward admitted, "Hell, I'm no financial genius. I know that." This was hardly a revelation to him; he'd proved it once before, when he served nine months in the state pen in 1939 for passing bad checks.

Fred Ward was a large, outgoing fellow, perfectly suited for life as a car salesman. A *Rocky Mountain News* columnist called him "the rotund, smiling car salesman [who] was a go-getter in charity drives, an entertainer of executives, a social climber of skill and charm."

Fred Ward was a dynamic car salesman whose Hudson dealership
in Denver was the largest in the West. When his company was
exposed as "a mirage," he admitted, "Hell, I'm no financial genius."

Courtesy of *The Denver Post*

He enjoyed his extravagant lifestyle. He was chairman of the American Heart Association and a successful bidder on prize-winning animals at the National Western Stock Show, frequently throwing open his twenty-three room mansion in suburban Broomfield for fund-raising events, and donating new Hudsons to numerous charity auctions. He loved to gamble, sometimes dropping $1,100 on one roll of the dice. He spent $120,000 on the 152-acre spread in Adams County, where he raised cattle and thoroughbred horses and entertained politicians and business partners poolside. He jokingly referred to the Hilltop Acres ranch as "Poverty Point."

But there was another side to the happy backslapper: He was a liar. He liked to tell people that he was born in Virginia in 1908 and orphaned at the age of ten when his mother, father, and older brother died in a typhoid epidemic. He claimed he was a star athlete in high school and went to the University of Michigan on an athletic scholarship for three years before he was forced to leave school during the Depression to take a job as a theater manager. He arrived in Denver in 1933 with one dollar in his pocket, he said, and spent his first night in town sleeping in his car (or sometimes it was, in his telling, under a tree) in City Park.

Almost all of it was made up. An exposé written by Bert Hanna in *The Denver Post* in July 1952, when Ward's financial empire was under fire, revealed that his real name was Fred Allen Williams and that his parents were, in fact, still alive. "Danged if I know why he went under that name," his father, E. Fred Williams, told the reporter.

The actual saga of Ward's early life was not as gripping as he made it out to be. State records showed that he never went beyond the eighth grade and never enrolled at Michigan. And, it seems, he neglected to mention that in 1933, the year he moved to Denver, he left behind a wife, Maxine, a baby daughter, Betty Ann, and an IOU for $840 that vanished from the safe at the theater he managed. Ward also overlooked the fact that, due to legal complications, he wasn't divorced from Maxine when he married for a second time in Colorado.

The vagabond Ward's first job in Denver was as a traveling salesman for a woolen-goods firm. He got married, went to work selling cars for the Thomas-Hickerson Motor Company, and in only two years was the top Dodge salesman in the Rocky Mountain region. Buoyed by his success, he borrowed money from friends—an ongoing habit that eventually would land him in prison—to open his own used-car lot at Twentieth and Welton Streets. He was so successful at it that Hudson offered him a dealership in 1945, and he quickly became the distributor for seventy-three dealers in six states.

America was car mad after the rationing days of World War II. When the war ended in 1945, millions of soldiers returned to civilian life and wanted the goods and services they had fought to defend. Suburbs boomed as young families grew and breadwinners needed automobiles to get to and from work and to enjoy weekend outings. At the same time, thousands of servicemen and servicewomen who had passed through Colorado during their war years found it a place they wanted to live. They were a perfect target for Ward and his salesmanship.

Ward's dealership was flying high. In 1947, it logged $1,364,050 in sales. The next year it rose to $1,682,216, jumping to $8,966,371 in 1949 and $8,405,601 in 1950. Hudson was twelfth in sales nationally, but in Ward's territory, it ranked third.

The 200-pound Ward knew how to live as a large as his girth. He barreled through life at an extravagant speed. His two-story Hudson dealership at Thirteenth Avenue and Lincoln Streets (later the home of Colorado Ballet) featured a luxurious office with a huge desk, walnut paneling, leather chairs, and a fully stocked bar.

But time was running out on the joyous, high-flying "life." There were warning signs in late 1950 that the company, and Ward, were in financial trouble.

In March 1951, Ward partnered with O. E. "Smiling Charlie" Stephens, a notorious gambler and former convict. Stephens testified in Ward's bankruptcy hearing in August that he gave US National Bank a list of 128 cars he purchased for Ward for $278,546.26. In exchange, Stephens would receive a $50 to $100 "premium" on each car sold. All but twenty-six were resold to dealers in Colorado, Wyoming, and New Mexico. The bank's attorneys checked Stephens's cars against the bank's list of 255 cars on which Ward owed $476,601. "We found, as we had expected, that many of the cars Stephens had loaned money on were cars we had previously loaned on," said the bank's attorney. Stephens had a hunch something was up when he went to cash one of Ward's checks and was told there were no funds to cover it.

On August 1, 1951, Fred A. Ward Inc. went into receivership. A court-appointed receiver reported that the company indebtedness topped $3 million with assets of only $732,000. The financial wolf pack descend-

Fred Ward's Hudson dealership

Author's collection

ed on Ward and his company. In September, a grand jury returned twelve indictments containing thirty felony charges against him. US National Bank, which carried Ward through numerous overdrafts, some as large as $100,000, closed on eight overdue promissory notes. The bank claimed that it had loaned Ward money on the dealer's pledge of 255 new Hudsons when the company had only 122 on hand.

Worse, said Stephens, Ward still owed him $62,000. He denied on the stand, however, that he had "roughed up" Ward to extract payment. Investigators got a tip that twenty-seven of the missing autos were hidden in a barn at Stephens's ranch near Littleton, south of Denver. No cars were found. Stephens explained that for convenience he had moved the cars to a garage at East Eighteenth Avenue and Pearl Street, but when Ward's troubles went public he went to check on them. They were gone.

A hard rain was falling on Ward and his dealership. The biggest mystery was what had become of his stock of automobiles. Mostly, it didn't exist. Scrambling to cover his assets, Ward sold cars he didn't have, sold the same car several times, or took out loans with nonexistent stock as collateral.

Denver District Attorney Bert Keating filed a false-pretense suit against Ward, based on a complaint by H. E. Mai, owner of Mountain Motors, who said Ward had promised to furnish Mai with five new Hudsons, for which he gave Ward a $5000 check. He never got the cars, and when he asked for his money back, Ward gave him a personal check that bounced.

Things were spiraling out of control. Checks to seventy of Ward's employees bounced, then they got no checks at all. Pete Smythe, a well-known radio personality who handled public relations for the dealership, was out two weeks' pay and a new Hudson that Ward had loaned him, which was confiscated in the bankruptcy.

Colorado governor Dan Thornton, who had partied with other prominent politicians and businessmen at Wards's ranch, was pulled into the dealer's desperate scheme. He loaned Ward $10,000 with the promise of a $12,500 repayment, but the check bounced only days before the scandal went public. Thornton said ruefully, "I'm in the cattle business where you accept a man at his word. I thought Ward was a reputable dealer. I tried to cash Ward's check; it bounced. I have it over in my Gunnison ranch now, as a souvenir."

The list of creditors scrambling to get back at least part of what they were owed was extensive. There were items as large as $539,323.51 owed

Fred Ward and his wife, Iva, whom he married after their
third date when she was eighteen years old, testified after
a grand jury indicted him on thirty felony counts of false
pretenses and conspiracy. She thought him "magnetic."

Courtesy of *The Denver Post*

to Fred Ward Inc., and $235,000 to J. K. Mullen Corporation. There were myriad small items, too, including $6 to Colorado Pump & Supply Company, $44 to Deep Rock Water Company, and $30 to Neusteters Department Store. Mack and Bob, a tailoring store, wanted $1,784.20 for personal clothing.

Even Ward's drinking habits came under federal investigation. In November, Albert Gould, the court-appointed bankruptcy attorney, pounded away at Ward's testimony that his liquor bills were both a legitimate business expense and tax deductible. The government didn't buy it.

> GOULD — *Here's an item for $648 paid to a Denver drug store. What was that for?*
> WARD — *Whisky.*
> GOULD — *Did you benefit personally by this purchase?*
> WARD — *No, sir. Other than drinks I had with customers.*
> GOULD — *What was the liquor for?*
> WARD — *Well, let's see. If I remember correctly, that purchase was made for a Christmas party the company gave employees. We maintained a bar in my office at the company. We gave customers and visiting Hudson factory representatives drinks. Around Christmas our liquor bills were high. We gave customers whisky, we had employee parties, we gave bottles away to dealers who conducted business with us, and we passed out case after case for Christmas presents.*

The government also questioned business expenses for jewelry, shrubbery, frequent plane trips, clothing, and the purchase of prize-winning cattle, hogs, and sheep. All these, Ward explained, were for the benefit of Fred A. Ward Inc.

During his trial, Ward was forced to take to his bed at his ranch mansion, sidelined by severe chest pains and extreme high blood pressure. For a time, he was under heavy sedation. Newspapers said he "may be dead by morning," a claim his lawyer made it a point to refute.

Ward's wife, Iva, wrote an as-told-to article in *Empire*, the Sunday magazine of *The Post* in October 1951 in which she described the couple's early life together: "Fred Ward asked me to become his wife on our third date. I was eighteen years old at the time. (Ward was twenty-six.) We were married six weeks later on New Year's Day 1935 in Pueblo, Colorado." Ward's divorce from his first wife wasn't final until 1939.

Iva was working as a waitress, "but not a good one. I couldn't serve a cup of coffee without spilling it." The whirlwind romance was easy to explain, she said. "Fred's magnetic, almost hypnotic influence on me. He never was a handsome man but there's a power to him." She considered divorcing him when he went to prison in 1939 for passing bum checks but couldn't bear to part with him.

Iva lamented, "When the news broke about the collapse of Fred Ward Inc., and Fred Ward the man, everything went to pieces. We had to lock the gates, keep constant guard against the people who wanted to loot our place. They tried to steal cattle, produce, everything. They came to the door wanting to snoop through our house. They picked our flowers, which were my special pride."

She admired that her husband never called it quits. During the worst of the bankruptcy hearings, he proposed to his creditors that he be allowed to run his ranch as an upscale supper club to pay off his debts. His spread would become an elegant club, offering food, drinks, entertainment, tennis, swimming, horseback riding, golf, and trout fishing. The federal referee in the hearing wanted no part of that.

On August 25, 1952, Judge Joseph J. Walsh sentenced Ward to seven to fifteen years, with a minimum of four years, in state prison for a confidence game, false pretenses, and two counts of conspiracy. In passing sentence, Walsh said, "It is an enigma to this court why this crime was ever committed." Ward declined comment. His legal troubles weren't over. In November 1953, he pleaded guilty to two federal grand jury indictments charging him with using the mails to defraud, which added another year to his term.

In November 1952, just before he was sent by car from Denver to the state penitentiary in Cañon City, Colorado—along with four other prisoners and accompanied by guards—Ward was still unbowed. "I could have pulled my business out of the hole if they had let me alone. I'm still confident that if they'd gone along with me I could have saved my business and paid back every cent I owe."

Ward, who converted to Catholicism while incarcerated, returned to Denver in 1959 after his parole from the federal McNeil Island Prison in Puget Sound, Washington, having served six years and three months behind bars.

From a high-flying automobile dealer to an inmate at
the state penitentiary in Cañon City, Fred Ward resumed
his old job in the prison kitchen, where he worked after
he was convicted of check fraud in 1939.

Courtesy of *The Denver Post*

Give the expansive Ward this: He was no quitter. When he went behind the stone walls of the state penitentiary he vowed, "I'll pay back my creditors every cent that I owe. And I'll make a comeback in business."

A dramatic return to the business world seemed far away when he went through the same routine all new prisoners did—a shower, his head shaved—and given a number, 27398. First he was assigned to the prison's infamous rock pile; then, for good behavior, he was moved to the kitchen where he peeled potatoes and washed dishes—ironically, the same chores he performed during his 1939 stay.

On his release, he almost immediately went to work on a new moneymaking scheme, one he predicted would make him a million dollars and enable him to pay back every penny he owed. He invented, with the help of another prisoner, the Fred Ward Nylon Washer, a plastic football–sized device that women could fill with soapy water and shake to wash their nylons. Ward claimed he had orders for 700,000 balls, which sold for $1.69. He had other inventions, too—a dripless saucer, which cleverly caught any drips from a cup in a depression; "Nylergence," a detergent to be used in his plastic ball; and a plastic toe cap to protect boys' shoes from wear. There was a safety device "that will teach children how to cross busy streets safely." His idea for a quick-frozen baked potato died before it got out of the planning stages when a California company beat him to it by eight months. He put together a company, with his wife as president, that manufactured children's wood furniture using prison labor. None of these endeavors ever came close to making the kind of money Ward needed to dig himself out of his financial hole.

Heart problems, which plagued Ward for much of his life, finally caught up with him when he died of a heart attack on March 11, 1962, at the age of fifty-four, in a Dallas motel while he was on a business trip with his wife for their playground equipment company. A popular rumor at the time was that he choked to death on a piece of steak, but his son, Gene, confirmed that it was a heart attack.

Today, Ward's one-time ranch, the scene of so many parties and happy times, is part of a commercial, industrial, and residential development at West 120th Avenue and Interstate 25 in Broomfield. The ebullient car dealer's mansion serves as the clubhouse for the Front Range Country Club. He would have gotten satisfaction that his plan for such a country club finally came to fruition.

CHAPTER 13

THE PRINCE AND THE SOCIALITE

JANE TOMBERLIN

It was love at first sight between the well-known Denver society woman and the dashing Hawaiian prince. Or, more accurately, love at first elevator ride.

He was His Highness Samuel Crowningburg-Amalu, the chief Kapiikauinamoku, Prince of Keawe. In the series of bizarre events that followed, he immediately became "Prince Sam" to headline writers at Denver's two daily newspapers, which sniffed that he was the "Elevator Romeo." The son of a car dealer on the islands, Sam, thirty-six, had good looks with dark-brown eyes, stood six feet tall, and was a stocky 190-pounder. His thinning black hair was combed straight back, his frequent smile revealed three gold-capped teeth, and he oozed charm with a clipped British accent cultivated in his travels through Europe. His adventures often were fueled by Cutty Sark and ginger ale.

She was Jane Tomberlin, forty-seven, ex-wife of a millionaire Denver oilman, who lived at the lavish Brown Palace Hotel when not at her alternate home in Hawaii. Her previous marriage was to Bill Tomberlin, a six-foot-six oilman whom she married in 1948 in Rawlins, Wyoming, not long after he struck a well that produced 130 barrels a day and made him rich. The couple visited Hawaii frequently and lived in Cherry Hills, a well-to-do suburb of sprawling mansions south of Denver, where he became a golfing buddy of President Dwight Eisenhower, a frequent guest

Jane Tomberlin

Rocky Mountain News, courtesy of the Western History and Genealogy Department, Denver Public Library

at the Brown. The Tomberlins divorced in 1953, and she was awarded a tidy $3-million settlement.

Her warp-speed romance with the prince began with an "Aloha!" on an elevator at the Brown. She thought—accurately it turned out—that he might be Hawaiian. It was a one-week leap from a casual conversation to wedding bells. They might have taken their cue from *Love Me Tender*, Elvis Presley's first motion picture, which debuted in New York City that month.

The couple decided to marry on November 28, 1956; it would be her fourth. Everything was arranged. Denver district judge Albert T. Frantz would perform the ceremony in his chambers at 2:30 p.m., with the reception to follow at the prince's suite in the Brown Palace. Mrs. Tomberlin was outfitted in a silk Chinese-style, knee-length dress with a scoop neckline. The guests included several well-known names from Denver's social elite and friends who had flown in from California.

Everyone was there.

Except the groom.

No word from his highness, who was supposed to be hurrying back from Dallas where he was on business. After an awkward lapse, Jane went ahead with the reception, flowing with canapés, pineapple, poi, and lots and lots of champagne. She was not, however, pleased. "I'm damned mad," she told a reporter, but she declined to answer any questions about the prince's disappearing act and the "wedding mix-up."

Amalu returned to Denver three days later and had an explanation for his absence: His brother, who opposed the marriage, had kidnapped him. He ended up, he said, in "some strange place, some cow ranch deep in south Texas. I hate cows. I can't tell a cow from a bull."

Some were disbelieving. Although Prince Sammy claimed, "It seems every time I marry, my family disagrees," a friend said the prince simply had gotten cold feet. Jane's faith in Sam was unshaken, however—"Sam will come back to me." She also cooed that the prince "is dashing, a perfect gentleman, a wonderful dancer and possessed of a good sense of humor. He used to say, 'You Jane, me Tarzan.'"

All being forgiven, the happy couple tried the wedding vows again on November 30, this time at the Antlers Hotel in Colorado Springs, with Jane's friend Mrs. Carleton Potter as matron of honor and Mike Cobb, manager of the Antlers, as best man. Sam bought her a $7.50 wedding band at the hotel's gift shop. The honeymoon took them no farther than the General Palmer Suite at the Antlers, a comfortable $82.50-a-day accommodation.

The honeymoon was cut short because Amalu, along with his business manager, his secretary, and his driver, were tossed into the El Paso County Jail on investigation of fraud. The prince's "entourage" was a ragtag group. Arrested with him were Walter Parman, twenty-four, his secretary; Frederick Aykens, forty-four, his business manager; and James Darnell, seventeen, his chauffeur. Only a month earlier, police said, Parman had been an aircraft mechanic. Aykens, a draftsman, had been the prince's business manager for a week, and Darnell said he was a high school student hired as a driver just two weeks prior.

The arrests, made as Sam and Jane were exiting the Antlers, were awkward. Jane fled town in tears, but not before she paused to dictate a letter to Bishop National Bank in Honolulu to stop payment on a $2,800 check she had given Sam.

The prince's playboy lifestyle was quickly disintegrating. A disturbing report in the *Honolulu Star-Bulletin* said the self-proclaimed royal heir was no such thing. An expert in Hawaiian royal genealogy wrote that the Hawaiian monarchy expired in the 1890s, that Prince Sam certainly was no "high chief," and that there is no such title as Prince of Keawe. Like many Hawaiians, however, he was distantly related to the royal family.

Shaken, Jane announced that she would seek an annulment to end the marriage because she was "suffering extreme grief and disappointment and I'm convinced I was the victim of a con game." Besides, she added, the marriage was never consummated.

In San Francisco, there was the unresolved matter of a $45,000 check the prince had scribbled as the down payment on a honeymoon home he bought sight unseen. The check bounced. In the following days, it came out that Amalu had served two years in a Philippine prison for swindle and was deported to Hawaii in 1954.

Right behind the Colorado Springs officials came agents of the FBI, looking into complaints from the Brown Palace Hotel that the prince had left behind $600 of bum checks during his stay. This was on top of the unpaid balance of $1,300 for the couple's bill at the Antlers.

While Amalu was explaining his embarrassing shortage of funds and promising that he had $3 million in a Hong Kong bank that he just couldn't get his hands on, Jane took off for Honolulu. The prince's love

Prince Amalu and his new bride, Jane Tomberlin, were all smiles
after their marriage at the Antlers Hotel in Colorado Springs.
The couple decided to wed a week after they met on
an elevator at the Brown Palace Hotel.

Rocky Mountain News, courtesy of the Western History and Genealogy Department, Denver Public Library

was undiminished. "Will I try to win her back? I don't have to. She's still my wife, isn't she? I still love her, and I'm sure she still loves me. As far as I am concerned, nothing has changed between me and Jane. I know we love each other." The prince fell in love often—ultimately, he would be married five times, twice to the same woman.

When Amalu was arrested, he left behind him a string of dazzled hotel employees. He'd charmed waiters, elevator girls, and the manager of the Antlers. He'd kissed hands; he knew how to order elaborate meals but preferred lobster and steak. He'd sprung for champagne at the Broadmoor Hotel tavern so the orchestra would play Hawaiian tunes while he and his friends took off their shoes and danced the hula. Colorado Springs police chief I. B. "Dad" Bruce marveled, "The prince is the nicest talker I've ever met. Reminds me, I have to go out and buy him some cigarettes."

Author and longtime friend Kathleen Melley from his Honolulu hometown told the press after their meeting at a cocktail party that he "has an utterly wonderful imagination" and "I was entranced. He was very handsome." She saw only his sunny side. She was quoted in a 1971 biography, *Sammy Amalu: Prince, Pauper or Phony?*:

> *He's magnificent. What a majestic gesture ... a grand contribution he's made to this world that's torn by strife and tension. Why just think of the boldness and the imagination—that he would return to our hometown to bamboozle—put it that way, it's a good term for it—a group of prominent citizens. He hasn't done anyone any harm. He doesn't go after the poor people. Never. Leave him free to go his blithe and merry way.*

Amalu, for all his charm and language skills, was now facing multiple federal charges, including mail fraud, transporting forged checks across state lines, and using interstate communications in a scheme to defraud the Brown Palace by sending telegrams for reservations to the hotel, then asking the hotel to forward his unpaid bills to a bank in San Francisco. Despite these mounting charges, Amalu never blinked. During his trial, he told reporters that money was no problem. "In actual cash, I suppose, I'm probably worth $500,000 and in property, something in excess of that."

Nevertheless, the man who relished steak and lobster spent his thirty-seventh birthday and Christmas in the local jail, dining on a holiday meal of chicken, the same meal all inmates received.

Meanwhile, Jane couldn't make up her mind about her dashing, erstwhile love. In January 1957 she dropped her annulment suit. "It must be true love," sighed her attorney. In March, she and the prince walked out of the US Marshal's office arm in arm after she posted a $10,000 cash bond for his release from Denver County Jail. They set up, not at the Brown, but at the slightly lower-brow Cosmopolitan Hotel across Broadway.

In June, a jury of seven women and five men in federal district court found Sam and two of his aides (his seventeen-year-old chauffeur was spared) guilty of ten counts of conspiracy and using interstate wire facilities to defraud hotels in Colorado and Texas as well as the Hong Kong and Shanghai Bank of San Francisco. Each of the men received a four-year sentence at Leavenworth Prison.

In his bristling closing statement, prosecutor Robert Wham said, "There is no truth to his story of wealth in the Far East. He has told a confusing and unbelievable story. It's been five months and the hotels are still unpaid. Where is this immense wealth?" Sitting in the front row of the audience, Jane closed her eyes as the verdict was read.

By August, she'd had enough of the pretend prince. She filed for divorce even though he told the world that she sent him love letters daily to his cell. In fact, he said, he encouraged her to get a divorce because "I'll be in for three years, and that's not a very pleasant prospect for a woman. [She's] a wonderful woman. I think very highly of her." The divorce was finalized on October 16, 1960, and she dropped out of the Denver social scene.

The prince was released from Leavenworth on September 8, 1960, but his legal troubles were far from over. In his past were thousands of dollars in bum checks floating around. When he motored through Honolulu in his white Lincoln Continental and dazzling all-white outfits, he bought gas with somebody else's credit card. One day after his release from Leavenworth, he was arrested by FBI agents in Portland, Oregon, for violating his parole and was sent to McNeil Island Correctional Center in Puget Sound, Washington, to serve another five months.

In 1962, Amalu became involved in the grandest of all of his wild schemes—a syndicate called the International Trade Exchange Central, allegedly in negotiation to buy four Sheraton hotels at Waikiki Beach for $34.5 million. There were purported offers from him and others to buy a Molokai ranch for $5 million, a sugar plantation, and plans to build a

His Highness Samuel Crowningburg-Amalu, Chief Kapikauinamoku,
Prince of Keawe, also known to reporters as "Prince Sam,"
left a string of bounced checks and unpaid hotel bills in his wake.
One police chief called the handsome Hawaiian
"the nicest talker I ever met."

Author's collection

movie studio, hotels, and office buildings. These deals, if they'd material-ized would have been worth about $50 million in all.

Amalu loved pulling scams, especially on well-to-do businessmen. A woman acquaintance offered an explanation: "Amalu says the reason he does these things is that he likes to put things over on people—that's the way he gets his kicks." Asked to comment, a psychiatrist said of him, "He sowed the seeds of his own destruction."

The prince collected odd friends, and wasn't above defrauding them, too. Three young men, all surfers, were drawn into his empty scheme to purchase the Sheraton properties after he promised them clothes, money, and a new car each. They fell in with Amalu's circle of wealthy acquain-tances on the islands. They were supposed to be paid a couple of thousand dollars a month as "pro-regents" (Amalu's aides), but never got a penny and finally threw up their hands and left for the mainland. One of them said later, "Everything always seemed to be a big joke to Sam—he was always playing jokes on the press and everyone. He was always trying to keep the press running around and baffled, and was constantly on the telephone with the newspapers."

The Sheraton deal fell apart when the hotel's holding company dis-covered that one of the partners turned out to be none other than Prince Amalu, a convicted felon. Sheraton officials were embarrassed by the hoax. One of them admitted, "This hasn't cost us any money, but it looks like we're going to have to live with the laughs for some time to come."

Hotel executives were waiting in New York City to finalize the deal when word came that Amalu had been arrested in Seattle. A lawyer named George T. Davis, who also happened to be a fugitive on two bad-check warrants in San Francisco, had signed complaints that Sam had written a bad check for $30,000 for an option on the ranch on Molo-kai and, on top of that, wrote a personal check to Davis for $200 that bounced.

Amalu never missed a beat and still regarded Davis as "a friend." In a letter that was equal parts tortured reasoning and outright blarney, he wrote:

> I am, of course, aware of your repute in the specific field of law, and I assure you I am in need of competent counsel. ...
> I realize, however, that it would be somewhat unusual for you to represent me in that particular case wherein you yourself are the complaining witness. This would produce a paradox in that the only

way you could possibly win would by losing—and contrarily, you by losing would win. Such, I am certain, would test your own native acumen and would be a challenge of no mean proportion.

Davis responded coldly, "I certainly do not represent him." Amalu got a year at Folsom Prison in California for his latest frauds.

While he was behind bars, he took up writing a controversial column for the *Honolulu Advertiser*, a role he continued until 1984. The columns generally consisted of Amalu's flowery five-and-dime philosophies of life and living behind bars, writings that even he called "fluff." His work did, however, give him time to think about his life—self-serving, grandiose thoughts he was happy to share:

I do admit that there are times when I wish I might have been the kind of son for which my parents truly hoped. In my life I have hurt a lot of people. Certainly not intentionally. And never with malice. But this may really be the worst way to hurt people.

I have sometimes been extremely careless of the hearts that I loved best, and this is a great cruelty for it spells indifference.

Oh, yes, there are some things that I wish had been otherwise. But this wishing too is a part of life and living.

"The Nureyev of con men" even wrote his own obituary, which appeared in the *Advertiser* after he died at age sixty-nine in 1986:

Sing no sad songs over my mortal dust. I have known laughter. I have known tears. I have tasted victory. I have sipped of failure. Is not all this enough?

CHAPTER 14

THE MAN WHO COULD DO NO WRONG

PASTOR CHARLES E. BLAIR

> Pride goeth before destruction, and
> an haughty spirit before a fall.
> —Proverbs 16:18

If Pastor Charles E. Blair had paid more attention to the Good Book and less attention to cooking the books, his life might have turned out very differently.

Blair, who began his religious life in Denver with a minuscule congregation, was flying high by the 1960s. He was preaching to 6,000 adherents, with three services every Sunday at the interdenominational Calvary Temple, and reaching almost 100,000 people with his weekly television and radio shows. His church's popularity had risen to the point that Calvary ranked third in attendance among Denver attractions, out-drawn only by the Denver Zoo and the Museum of Natural History.

Pastor Blair was as high profile as his church. He took pleasure in hobnobbing with his fellow men of the cloth and counted among his friends evangelists Oral Roberts and Pat Robertson—both of whom campaigned to help him raise money—and entertainer Pat Boone. The well-dressed, slightly built minister who always seemed to be smiling was a charismatic charmer. "He's a super salesman," said one who knew him. "He could sell the pants off of anybody, and he knows how to use publicity."

Blair was one of the first among his brethren in the pulpit to realize the power of radio and television to attract followers and cash. Beginning in 1967, he hosted a daily thirty-minute radio show called *Prayertime* that ended with the words, "Smile, Look Up—and Trust!" His Sunday sermon, "The Calvary Temple Hour," was carried live on local television station KBTV Channel 9 and aired in eight states.

Thanks to his organizational and fund-raising skills, his empire expanded to embrace three entities—the Charles E. Blair Foundation, Calvary Temple, and Life Center—but it would take financial sleight-of-hand to keep all three operating. That's where the trouble began.

Born dirt-poor in Kansas in 1921, Blair and his family moved to Enid, Oklahoma, when he was a boy. Times were tough. To help support the family, he sold newspapers on the street, was a delivery boy for a drugstore, and sold magazines door to door. He once joked to his wife, Betty, "We were what the poor people called poor." He later wrote in his autobiography, ironically titled *The Man Who Could Do No Wrong*, that his hardscrabble early life had caused his almost fanatical drive for financial success.

Believing he'd been "touched by God" at a revival meeting as a youth, he attended Southwestern Seminary in Enid and North Central Bible School in Minneapolis and was ordained in the Assemblies of God Church in 1942. He bounced around as an itinerant minister for several years; then, in 1947, at the age of twenty-six, he was called upon by members of the Central Assembly Church at East Fourth Avenue and Grant Street in Denver to lead them out of a religious and financial wilderness. The church's then-membership of fifty-eight didn't come close to filling its 500-seat auditorium.

Blair's organizational and spiritual skills became apparent immediately. The church quickly outgrew its meager facility, built an addition, and purchased a nearby apartment building. Membership swelled to 1,200, and three Sunday services were required to handle the crowds.

That's when he hatched the idea of a "megachurch" with a magnificent new edifice grand enough to hold the energetic minister and his ambitious ideas. He cast around for a suitable location and bought up a string of small houses near East First Avenue and University Boulevard, a central location on two busy streets, but the Sears department store chain was wanting to build a new outlet in Cherry Creek and needed that same land. Sears got what it wanted, but so did the pastor.

God's guiding hand led him to a weed-strewn nine-acre plot at South University Boulevard and East Alameda Avenue. The Cherry Creek area was not the shopping and dining mecca it is today. The popular Cherry Creek Mall stands on a former dump and on the site of a shopping center conceived of in 1946 by noted architect Temple Buell on land he was farsighted enough to purchase in 1925.

Blair recounted in his autobiography how, amid the weeds and debris, he decided it was the place for his new church:

> *I was driving home along University Boulevard when my eyes were drawn to a large vacant meadow. I pulled the car to the curb and sat staring at it, ten acres at least of untouched and level land.*
>
> *I got out of the car and tramped through the tall weeds in the fading light, my heart thumping strangely against my ribs. How was it possible that our committees could have passed this lovely field without seeing it? Clearly the reason none of us had ever noticed this property was that it was too big, too beautiful, too far above our highest sights. But the thought now hammering wildly against my chest was: "Calvary Temple will stand here."*
>
> *As darkness fell I got down on my knees in that tall grass: "Lord, if this is your voice, let me not be afraid to listen."*

He wasn't afraid to listen. Ground was broken on the new, modernistic Calvary Temple on November 8, 1953, and the dedication service took place on June 26, 1955, with 2,500 attendees: capacity at the magnificent new structure of glass, steel, and stained glass, with its prow pointed toward heaven (and University Boulevard).

As it would often be, money was a problem. As part of a land swap with Sears, the church was given $68,000 by the department store. "The check from Sears and the sale of the church at Fourth Avenue and Grant Street would barely pay for the foundation," Blair wrote. "And so we did

Pastor Charles Blair ran his thriving religious empire from
Calvary Temple in Cherry Creek. Before its collapse,
the church with its ambitious pastor grew to 6,000
weekly parishioners and fifty-three employees, ten pastors,
and eighty-five missionaries worldwide.

Courtesy of *The Denver Post*

what churches all over the country were then doing with great success: we sold bonds. We sold our bonds first to ourselves, then we divided into teams and sold them to friends, neighbors, eventually to total strangers." It was a fund-raising technique that would eventually get Blair and his associates crosswise with securities investigators and the legal system.

But for the time being it was all blessed sunny skies. The church grew to fifty-three employees, ten pastors, twelve choirs and choral groups, and supported eighty-five missionaries worldwide.

Ever ambitious, Blair unveiled plans in March 1965 to convert the vacant Spears Chiropractic Hospital at East Eighth Avenue and Jersey Street into a 400-bed medical facility to be called Life Center, opening in January 1967. The 250,000-square-foot hospital and senior living center, Blair announced at a downtown hotel, would have a payroll of up to 1,800 doctors, nurses, and other personnel. There would be psychiatric services, surgery, obstetrics, emergency treatment, laboratories, and X-ray facilities and, eventually, apartments for seniors. His grand plan would come true but not until well after his death. In 2015, the Rosemark at Mayfair Park development virtually duplicated Blair's vision, with four apartment buildings and plans to add an assisted living and memory care center.

Life Center was another of Blair's expansive schemes. He told a gathering of clergymen and doctors that he dreamed of visiting an unfinished building just at the time the Spears family decided to sell the derelict property. To pay for the rebirth, expected to cost $6.25 million, organizers would sell ten-year bonds at 7 percent interest.

Seven years later, Calvary Temple and its pastor launched a $5-million expansion program that included a $1.4-million youth building, a 1,700-car parking lot, and plans for a new sanctuary capable of seating up to 5,000. The church already operated a preschool, kindergarten, and first grade, but he envisioned a full twelve-grade school in the new facility.

The first rumblings of trouble surfaced in 1971 when Warren Charles, a former Life Center attorney, raised red flags about financial problems. Blair and other church leaders ignored warnings, he said. But it wasn't until the spring of 1974 that the Colorado Securities Commission sought to have Calvary Temple, the Charles E. Blair Foundation, and Life Center, Inc. placed in receivership because, it said, the corporations were financially unstable and could face heavy losses. The three entities borrowed liberally from each other.

The commission charged that Calvary Temple sold securities of more than $4 million, the Blair Foundation sold securities in excess of $1 million, and sales by Life Center topped $6.5 million. Further, the commissioners said, the three organizations were selling time-payment or call-payment securities, even though their employees weren't licensed to sell securities, and that the sales techniques were "controlled and dominated by Blair." Debt was systemic. Calvary Temple had debts of $8.2 million; Life Center, $13.9 million; and the Charles E. Blair Foundation, $1 million.

A court-appointed commission recommended that the enterprises either be declared bankrupt or placed in court receivership with debts of $23.38 million, about $5 million more than their assets. "People have been defrauded out of their life savings," said district court judge Robert Kingsley. It was the first time the word *defrauded* had been uttered in public about the far-flung Blair empire.

All three entities chose Chapter 11 bankruptcy in federal court on June 7, 1974. The ever-upbeat Blair told *The Denver Post*, "God will raise up an army of 1,500 men and women" to donate to save his three enterprises. "I know God has a plan for this church." In a column written for *Temple Times*, the church newspaper, he listed eight ways contributors could donate to Life Center. "We stand on the threshold of what I believe will be the most exciting, victorious year of our entire history."

In July, Blair and others testified in a US Bankruptcy Court hearing, where, as was to become his mantra, he denied any hand in the financial shenanigans. Subordinates, he said, made unsecured loans "without consulting me."

Many of his elderly followers prayed for financial redemption, as much for themselves as for Pastor Blair. One couple, the Cavetts—with the unlikely first names of Pollyanna and Strange—sold their house and gave up their life savings of $30,000 for a Life Center apartment they never got. Strange, seventy-four, suffered from Parkinson's disease, and his fifty-four-year-old wife had rheumatoid arthritis. Their investment "took twenty-four years of doing without and saving up so we could take care of ourselves and no one else would have to," said Mrs. Cavett.

Still, their faith didn't waver. "The church was about the Heavenly Father's business as far as preaching, work with young people, and the nursing home went, but the people running it overextended themselves," she said.

Dozens of others filed written claims. They were more confused than angry. One wrote, "What I'm wondering is when Pastor Blair is going to make a sacrifice. It would be the Christian thing to do." Another philosophized, "Perhaps the church might look now at staying with the Lord's work and not getting involved in financial wheeling and dealing."

The investors with the best hope of seeing any money back were those who bought Calvary Temple securities. Bankruptcy judge Glen Keller Jr. approved a plan under which 1,200 of them would be repaid $7.65 million with interest under an eleven-year plan that called for quarterly payments of at least $125,000. The judge felt that Blair and his church's record at raising funds made repayment a good bet. Blair vowed his only plan moving forward was "to pay off our creditors and investors."

Easier said than done. An estimated 3,400 investors, stricken with religious and high-interest fervor, were owed $11 million from the failed Life Center project. One of the attorneys called it "a general mess." Another $12 million was owed to area banks, savings and loan associations, and mortgage brokers.

There was a repayment plan, one that appeared more Pollyanna than Mrs. Cavett. Calvary Temple would sell most of its real estate holdings and borrow another $1 million to pay off the Life Center investors.

All these promises did not satisfy a Denver grand jury, which, in December 1974, after a three-month investigation, indicted Blair and the church's chief fund-raiser, Wendell Vance, on twenty-one counts of fraudulent sale of securities between December 7, 1971, and March 13, 1974, and of conspiracy.

Vance was executive vice president of Life Center. The organization's finances—described by *Denver Post* reporter Cindy Parmenter as "selling time-payment certificates to Peter so it could make interest payments to Paul"—were so convoluted that even Vance couldn't understand them. The man in charge of fund-raising admitted during his trial, "I didn't know anything about securities. All our sales materials were prepared by corporate lawyers and our accounting firm. I had no background or frame of reference in this area." He also said that all major decisions were deferred to Blair.

After a brief trial in November 1975, in which he represented himself, Vance was convicted on eleven counts of fraudulent sales of securities. He paid a $5,500 fine and was placed on probation for five years after completing an eighteen-month sentence in the Colorado State Reformatory.

Blair, who promised everyone they would be repaid, worked diligently and raised $3 million in donations through rallies in Colorado, Wyoming, Montana, North Dakota, South Dakota, and Nebraska. There was the attempted sale of his palatial Polo Grounds mansion, known as "The Castle," for $185,000. (It was valued at $2.7 million in 2013.) No dice, said a court-appointed receiver who called the sale "inequitable and not in the best interests of [Calvary Temple]." The sale of two other homes owned by the church in the exclusive neighborhood was approved.

Blair's drive for financial security, born in his impoverished childhood, extended to real estate. Calvary Temple sits close to the Polo Club, one of the city's fanciest neighborhoods. When the temple was up and running, Blair bought forty-six adjoining acres for high-rise apartments before neighborhood protests derailed the project. It later sold to a developer for $1.5 million as part of the church's settlement to repay investors.

The church owned several very expensive homes in the neighborhood, including on East Cedar Avenue. "The Castle," where Blair and his wife relaxed rent-free from the rigors of salvation at 2750 East Cedar was aptly named—a 10,000-square-foot, seven-bedroom, two-story Spanish-style 1930s mansion, complete with a soaring tower and set on one and a half acres of tree-shaded land just east of the church grounds. Blair took care of himself, too. He religiously, every Friday morning, stopped by his favorite barbershop for a trim, blow dry, manicure, and shoe shine.

The sell-off of assets scooped up almost all the church's properties. Eleven acres of undeveloped land along Cherry Creek South were sold for $1.5 million, less than some others bid but an immediate sale. Calvary sold an additional forty-two-acre Polo Club property at East Alameda Avenue and Steele Street for $1.8 million. Blair told reporters that 65 percent of it would go to repay bondholders. The rest would be divided between Life Center, the Blair Foundation, and church creditors. Leaving no fund-raising stone unturned, there was even a garage sale, made up of donated items as diverse as an elephant's foot ashtray to ice skates.

Blair went on trial in August 1976 on charges of failing to inform investors of Calvary Temple's looming monetary problems. Nineteen disillusioned investors, many of them elderly, took the stand to pour out their tales of disappointment. *The Post's* Parmenter wrote, "There was the gray-haired woman from Denver who said she invested $25,000. ... A retired woman from Pueblo who described her $30,000 invested. ... The widow from Littleton who had put in $15,000." One woman told the court, "We felt we would be serving the Lord if we invested our $25,000 in Life Center. We felt secure in putting it in the church because it was run by Christian people under the leadership of Pastor Blair."

Peter Willis, Blair's attorney, countered that under his leadership Blair's church gave millions to charity around the world. The pastor, he said, "has done nothing more than exhibit good faith" in those who gave him bad advice, the victim of his own trusting nature. For his part, the pastor denied any involvement in the sale of securities. "Any intelligent person knows I was not responsible for everything that happened."

The jury was not among those people. It took less than seven hours to find Blair guilty of seventeen counts of securities fraud on August 13, 1976. For once, Blair was not smiling. As the verdict was read, he buried his face in his hands. Like Gabriel's horn, both the *Rocky Mountain News* and *The Denver Post* trumpeted Pastor Blair's conviction with page-one banner headlines. "Pastor Blair Found Guilty," shouted the *News*. "Rev. Blair Guilty of Fraud," echoed *The Post*.

Three days after his conviction, Blair continued to maintain his innocence. "I know that the farthest thing from my mind was ever to defraud or hurt anyone. My whole life has been spent helping people and bringing healing to those in need."

In December 1976, district court judge Clifton Flowers handed Blair a sentence of five years' probation and a $12,500 fine. Each offense could have led to one to three years in the state penitentiary, but the judge reasoned that throwing the pastor behind bars would scuttle any hope investors had of recouping their losses. Afterward, Blair held an impromptu press conference in the hallway outside the courtroom and told reporters, "I haven't been afraid of anything in connection with this case for some time. God has been very gracious to me. I am very grateful to him for the strength he has given to help me endure this whole ordeal."

Even after his empire's plunge into bankruptcy in 1974, some members of Calvary Temple clung to their faith in him. He continued to preach to packed houses at the church. In June 1975, even when investigations into his foundations were piling up, 7,000 admirers gathered at Red Rocks Amphitheater to celebrate the pastor's twenty-eighth anniversary as Calvary's minister. It cost a dollar admission for the regular Sunday service and featured a performance by Metropolitan Opera bass Jerome Hines. Wearing a ruffled tuxedo shirt and a bow tie, with his wife,

Even after his conviction on seventeen counts of
securities fraud, the Calvary Temple faithful stood by
their pastor; 7,000 of them showed up at a tribute for him
and his wife, Betty, at Red Rocks Amphitheater.

Courtesy of *The Denver Post*

Betty, at his side, Blair basked in the adoration and cut a three-tiered caked adorned with sparklers.

Asked if the proceeds were ticketed to help retire the church's debt, associate pastor Gil Moegerle told a reporter, "Yes, part of it will go to that."

Four years later, more than 10,000 people attended a weekend Jesus Rocky Mountain Rally, sponsored by Calvary Temple, near Elbert, Colorado, on the prairies east of Denver. They were entertained by music and a speech from Blair. The crowd paid in $30,700 but expenses soared to $130,000. A collection raised another $10,000 and an anonymous donor ponied up $20,000.

Through it all, Blair tried to raise funds to repay the debts. In 1977, a federal bankruptcy judge approved a plan to pay back $9.5 million in claims against Life Center. The proposal called for $500,000 to be paid annually for the first two years of a twelve-year schedule, $750,000 annually during the next three years, and $1 million annually after that until the debt was retired.

Blair launched the "Second Mile Campaign" at a Sunday service in 1986, vowing to raise $4 million, to be used (it was hoped) to help pay off the remainder of what was owed to "distressed" investors. The congregation already had helped raise $10 million over ten years, and the amount of money owed had dwindled from $18 million to $2.2 million, thanks, in part, to the fact that many elderly investors simply forgave the debt or died.

Unfortunately, Second Mile raised only $1.7 million, far short of its goal. A group of investors, those still alive, filed suit, claiming Blair had reaped $2,323 from the campaign and that the church made off with $600,000 of the fund intended for distressed investors. Blair found himself back in court in December 1990, charged with theft. However, the judge forgave the $1.2 million still owed and the class-action suit was settled for $700,000.

Blair's reaction was the same as ever: "I did nothing wrong. I have nothing to worry about. I have never taken a dime that didn't belong to me—no under-the-table gifts. I'm not a hero, just a servant of the Lord." In the end, $1.5 million of the original debt simply faded away, never to be repaid.

In 1998, now seventy-seven years old and fifty years after he took over the little Central Assembly Church, Blair resigned from Calvary Temple but remained senior pastor. In a farewell to the congregation he

After his conviction for securities fraud, a chastened Charles Blair went on a retreat to the mountain resort of Vail and prayed among the aspen to reconnect with his faith. He resigned from the church in 1998 when he was seventy-seven but remained its senior pastor.

Courtesy of Duane Howell

said "God has made it clear" that it was time to move on, adding that he had "no intention of ever retiring as far as my call from God is concerned." The man who took a woebegone little congregation and built it into a religious behemoth died at age eighty-eight at his home on August 20, 2009.

In Blair's obituary for the weekly *Westword*, Alan Prendergast summed up the ambitious pastor's life: "Blair was equal parts shrewdness and obtuseness. He understood TV's power to extend the reach of his ministry long before most televangelists discovered toll-free numbers or powder-blue leisure suits. But Blair had a hard time putting brakes on his ambition or admitting when he had overreached."

CHAPTER 15

THE QUEEN OF QUALITY HILL

LOUISE SNEED HILL

"First you must have money. Then you must have the knowledge to give people a wonderful time."

Invaluable advice from Louise Sneed Hill because she had both, in spades. As arbiter of the Denver social scene for more than thirty years, she ruled with a soft countenance and a glove-encased iron hand.

She became the bride of Crawford Hill, heir to a vast Colorado mining fortune, in Memphis, Tennessee, on January 16, 1895. The newlyweds migrated to Denver, and it wasn't long before she began to gather around her the rich and elite of the burgeoning young city. Her husband, described by friends as shy and nonaggressive, was content to live quietly in his wife's shadow.

By 1908, she felt bold enough to produce the first edition of *Who's Who in Denver Society: A Social Guidebook*, in which she put the social players in their proper places. There were names, many names, bits of advice on clothing and beauty, and numerous "dos" and "don'ts." Mrs. Crawford Hill was the featured attraction. The frontispiece was a full-length photograph of her in the outfit, complete with what appears to be the top of a wedding cake perched on her head, that she wore when she was presented to the court of King Edward VII. The caption reads, "Mrs. Crawford Hill/The Arbiter of Denver Society."

Louise Hill went all out with her outfit when she was presented to the court of King Edward VII in 1907. The heavily brocaded, raspberry-colored velvet train she wore brought only $22.50 when it sold at auction in the Hill mansion in 1947.

Author's collection

There were lists—"The Smart Set," with Mr. and Mrs. Crawford Hill first; "Types of Denver Beauty," including Mrs. Crawford Hill; and "Worth Over a Million," fifty-five rich men, including Crawford Hill.

She also dished helpful hints in "About Getting Into Society." What, she warned, would keep you out (in addition to the obvious prejudices of the time):

- An evident desire to break in hurriedly
- An attempt to buy social position
- A lack of good sense, good breeding, or self-control
- An unfortunate disposition.

She might have looked in the mirror. She wasted no time establishing a beachhead in local society by lavishing Crawford's millions on balls, parties, and other entertainments. She was opinionated and sometimes didn't use good sense in her battles. She could, and did, exclude hopefuls from her inner circle.

And self-control? Her long and ultimately tragic affair with dashing young polo player and clubman Bulkeley Wells said otherwise.

Wells was the ultimate man-about-town. He stood six-foot-four with an athlete's body, was an outstanding polo player, and belonged to all the right clubs in Denver. He was a Harvard graduate, wealthy, easily conversant with everyone he met, and a respected hydroelectric/mining engineer.

Born in 1872, the handsome and energetic Wells, blessed with a full head of dark hair, large brown eyes, and an aquiline nose to rival that of John Barrymore, was a favorite among the younger set in Colorado Springs and Telluride, where he lived part time, and in Denver.

Wells cut a dashing figure in his blue-and-gold uniform as a young cavalry officer in the Colorado National Guard and, later, became a pivotal figure in the "mining wars" in Cripple Creek and Telluride at the turn of the twentieth century. As an adjutant general in the guard, Wells was in charge of rounding up striking union miners by the dozens and shipping them out of Telluride.

When, exactly, he became friends with Mrs. Crawford Hill isn't known, but around 1914, their friendship ripened into a long-running and remarkably open affair, despite the fact that both were married. It was common knowledge that Louise Hill had a full-length portrait of Wells and a smaller one of her husband hanging in the reception hall of her mansion. Crawford turned a blind eye to the affair.

Louise Hill stands at the bottom of the curving marble staircase in her twenty-two-room mansion at East Tenth Avenue and Sherman Street, the epicenter for Denver society and the exclusive "Sacred 36." The mansion's foyer was home to portraits of both her husband Crawford Hill and her paramour Bulkeley Wells.

Courtesy of the Western History and Genealogy Department, Denver Public Library, Harry Rhoads Collection, Rh-5816

Wells and the Crawford Hills were at the epicenter of Denver society, frequently attending parties and theater openings together, and private dinners at each other's homes. The Hill mansion at East Tenth Avenue and Sherman Street was the scene of gay gatherings where Wells often was in attendance. He, in turn, entertained with elaborate dinner parties in his rooms at the upscale Hotel L'Imperiale, which stood at 314 Fourteenth Street until it was demolished in 1962. Louise was a frequent guest at Wells's soirees, sometimes with Crawford, sometimes not.

In 1918, Bulkeley's wife, Grace, filed for divorce in Telluride, charging abandonment because he spent more time visiting his mining investments than he did her, although they did have four children together. The divorce would have far-reaching consequences for him because Grace's father cut off Wells's financing, and the young man was out as manager of the giant Smuggler-Union mine owned by his father-in-law in Telluride.

When Louise's husband died in 1922 at age fifty-seven, she thought Wells would propose marriage. He did, but not to her. Instead, he surprised Denver society, and Louise, by marrying in January 1923 twenty-five-year-old blonde divorcée Virginia Schmidt of Battle Mountain, Nevada, a woman twenty-six years his junior.

This was a bad idea. Louise, then fifty-eight years old, did not take the rejection well and vowed to get her revenge on the clubman. Wells suffered another financial blow when Mrs. Hill prevailed upon her hyper-rich friend Harry Payne Whitney, who, it is estimated, bankrolled Wells's mining adventures for between $8 million and $11 million, to pull the plug on Bulkeley's cash flow.

Bulkeley's world of wealth and fast times disintegrated. His plan to revive the legendary Comstock mine property in Nevada came to nothing, and bad investments and gambling debts pushed him to the brink of bankruptcy.

Despondent and fearful of becoming destitute, Wells penned a suicide note in which he wrote, "As a result of all my difficulties and worries my mind is bound to go. Nothing but bankruptcy is possible as far as my estate is concerned. Do what you can for Mrs. Wells." On May 26, 1931, he was in his office in San Francisco's Hobart Building and asked business associate Joseph O'Brien for a loan of $20. O'Brien went to the bank to get the money and returned to find Wells unconscious with a bullet wound in his head and an automatic pistol beside his body. As Wells lay dying, his friend, who shared office space with him, told police, "His friends killed him; they made him invest in bum stocks."

Louise has been portrayed as nonchalant about his death, but that fall she wrote to their mutual friend Harry Blackmer, living in Paris, "Of course you have heard all about Bulkeley Wells. Was that not dreadful?"

After Wells's death, Louise Hill's social lifestyle continued to flourish, and she didn't apologize for it. "It's my business to entertain," she told the *Rocky Mountain News*. "And that is very serious business, you know. The world needs entertainment as well as work." She was in the paper frequently, attending a party at a friend's house, opening night at the opera, a charity event at her mansion. Her name will forever be synonymous with the "Sacred 36," an exclusive gathering of society ladies who met to play whist at the mansion, where the seventy-two-foot-long drawing room was just spacious enough to hold nine tables of four players, hence the thirty-six.

Where the "sacred" name came from has been the object of speculation. In a 1986 article on the Hill legacy in *Colorado Homes & Lifestyles* magazine, Marilyn Griggs cited an unnamed newspaper interview in which Mrs. P. Randolph Morris responded to a question by saying, "Goodness, you'd think we were sacred, the way you were asking." The story was headlined, "Party at Mrs. Hill's for the Sacred 36."

One person who famously could not crack the facade of the Sacred 36 was Margaret Brown, who, thanks to the Broadway play and movie, became known to the world long after death as "Molly Brown." Mrs. Hill found her crude, too liberal politically, unschooled, "new money"—and on top of all that, she was Irish Catholic. They attended some of the same social gatherings, but it wasn't until Margaret attained nationwide attention for her heroics during the sinking of the *Titanic* that the iron gates of the Hill mansion swung open for her, welcoming Mrs. Brown as an honored guest.

Louise Hill was queen of all she surveyed. Beginning in 1911 she stood old-line Denver society on its head when she inaugurated daytime dances, accompanied by champagne, at her twenty-two-room mansion in the emerging Quality Hill neighborhood. It was a craze. New York society figure and dance addict Edward Tinker dazzled Louise and her friends with the latest steps—the Turkey Trot, the Bowery Slide, the Wiggle, the Bunny Hug, and the Grizzly Bear. There were dances in the morning, midday, and sometimes late into the night.

Handsome, accomplished polo player and well-known society figure Bulkeley Wells stole Louise Hill's heart. They carried on a very public affair until he married someone else.

Courtesy of Stephen H. Hart Library and Research Center, History Colorado, 90.314.127

Her love of the dance got her in hot water at the fashionable Denver Country Club when her friend Mrs. Lucius Foster took to the dance floor with a bout of abandonment and gave a vivid example of that new dance craze the Shimmy. She even shook her shoulders. Club members, especially the older ones, were horrified. Louise stuck up for the young woman, to the point of tearing down a club notice prohibiting such wanton behavior. She was suspended from the club.

Her raison d'être was keeping Denver society in line, but she did it with charm and grace. There was no denying her sense of fashion. Short and slightly built, she almost always appeared in black-and-white outfits and was never seen without a hat on her brunette coiffure or elbow-length gloves that disguised her small hands. In a 1917 profile, *The Denver Post* gushed, "She has the grace, the charm, the diplomacy, the personality, the wealth, the home and all the qualities of leadership necessary to unite society here."

She was a woman of strong opinions, and those who enjoyed basking in her social light paid homage. In 1931, she responded, through her secretary, to an invitation to join the American League to Abolish Capital Punishment with a sharply worded reply: "She is not in sympathy with the work you are doing, but, on the contrary, is definitely in favor of continuance of the law providing for capital punishment."

During World War I, she exchanged charges and countercharges in *The Post* with Captain John Evans over the issue of society women appearing at events clad in furs and expensive gowns instead of donating their wealth to the war effort.

In a bylined article—her father-in-law and her husband were both former owners of *The Denver Republican* newspaper so she was press savvy—she wrote, "May we not do more good by a smile or by bringing a little sunshine to those at home who are bearing the burdens, financially, economically, and industrially of the great conflict? We are giving in the war the best we have—our sons."

She had her stumbles. She was brought before a New Jersey magistrate in 1913 and fined $300 on a charge of smuggling after she was nabbed substituting American labels on two silk dresses and a coat purchased in Europe for $731, a common sleight of hand among the rich to avoid paying import duties.

In 1917, she started, with great fanfare, the Colorado Soldiers' Family Fund to help those whose breadwinners were away due to World

War I. "It was the least we who stay at home can do." It turned out to be unnecessary because the National Guard already had ordered soldiers with families to be discharged. She quickly donated the money gathered to the American Red Cross.

She was, to a point, an ardent suffragette. "I vote because I think it's the duty of women to vote as long as they have the ballot," she told an interviewer. "But I must confess I see no good that they have done in politics. Women are too emotional to hold public office."

Her opinion of men, especially men whose heads could be turned by an attractive, well-dressed woman, was harsh. "For women, after all, are cleverer than men," she wrote in a fashion article in *The Post* in 1917. "The stupidest woman I ever knew was cleverer than the cleverest man I ever knew. All a girl or woman needs to make herself attractive is to wash her face and comb her hair." She offered further advice to the fairer sex. "Some women in the matter of dress are roses and some are cabbages. Make up your mind that you won't be a cabbage."

She had a private, softer side. She threw numerous fund-raising events at the mansion for charities. When her longtime maid Cora Cowan was struck with appendicitis in 1916, Louise kept a vigil at her hospital bed and was with her when she woke up from surgery. Cowan, never married, helped raise Louise's sons Nathaniel and Crawford, crossed the Atlantic with Louise many times, and served the Hill household for more than twenty-five years. When Cowan died in April 1930, her funeral took place among a sea of flowers and the splendor of the Hill drawing room with many society figures in attendance. Louise lamented in a note to her good friend Helen Bonfils, daughter of *Post* owner Frederick Bonfils, "Cora's death is one of the greatest sorrows that ever came into my life."

She was strict with her two sons, both of whom enjoyed successful business careers in the East but didn't visit their mother in Denver often enough to keep her happy. To her younger son, Crawford, in Newport, Rhode Island, she complained, "The Boettchers ... said that you are so fat they would never have known you had someone at the table not told them who you were. That is a terrible grief to me, for you know how much I told you about growing fat." Later, she urged him to "get thin and stand up straight."

She regarded both sons as "chums," but her frustration with her son Crawford for not telling her that a friend was coming to visit the man-

Even in her later years, Louise Hill carried herself with a regal bearing. She closed down her mansion in 1944 and spent her declining
days in Apartment 904 at the Brown Palace Hotel, where she died
at midnight on May 28/29, 1955, at age ninety-four.

Courtesy of the Western History and Genealogy Department,
Denver Public Library, Harry Rhoads Collection

sion boiled over in a letter to him when she snapped, "You are the worst child I have ever had!"

There was one more bit of business concerning the turbulent relationship she'd had with her erstwhile lover, Bulkeley Wells. In 1932, Louise sold the home she owned and where Wells had lived at West Colfax Avenue and Cleveland Place to make way for construction of a filling station.

Ill health, which plagued Louise for years, began to get the best of her. In August 1937 she wrote to Crawford, "You see, my trouble is with my heart. In more than three weeks I have had one meal not in my bed. Everyone tells me that I am very brave about it all; as a matter of fact, I am not. I am frightfully depressed every day."

In another anguished letter written in 1940, she complained, "I lie here in this room practically all of the time, most of the time in abject agony. Fancy yourself lying on your back, alone, for a month, scarcely a human being to speak to."

That same year, she took a spill while stepping into her bathtub. She was taken to St. Luke's Hospital with a fractured shoulder and was still confined to the mansion the following February. The parties and the gaiety came to a halt.

In 1944, she shut down the mansion. For public consumption, the reason was difficulty in finding domestic help to run the huge place during World War II. The fact was that Louise's health was in precipitous decline. Finally, in October, at the age of seventy-nine, she moved to the Brown Palace Hotel.

Fading into senility, she lived out her last years in her ninth-floor suite at the Brown, attended to by a battery of nurses and rarely receiving visitors. She died near midnight on May 28, 1955, at the age of ninety, although newspaper obituaries at the time said she was ninety-four. She never discussed her age. When asked, she would reply, "I was born in North Carolina, where a girl becomes 16 when she's about 12 or 14. She stays 16 until she's 21 and she remains 21 until she's 30. Finally, she's 85, and then tells everyone she's 100."

The curtain fell on the Hill era at the exquisite 1905 mansion in 1947 when its contents and Mrs. Hill's personal belongings went under the auctioneer's hammer. Socialites, including old friends Eleanor Weckbaugh, Mrs. Charles MacAllister Willcox, Mrs. Henry C. Van Schaack, and Mrs. Harold Kountze, were among the hundreds crammed into the solarium when the sale began.

Items sold at rock-bottom prices. Twenty-six glass dinner plates went for $3; hundreds of books sold for $6 a box; three real-estate maps of Denver dating to 1871, 1874, and 1876 brought $1 each; and a massive French mahogany bed valued at $1,200 was a steal at $110. A sterling silver hairbrush bearing Mrs. Hill monogram was worth only $11. The greatest insult was when the sweeping ten-foot-long train of raspberry-colored velvet that Louise wore for her presentation at the British court was sold for $22.50. Local historian Caroline Bancroft, unwilling to see a piece of Denver history sold for such a pittance, paid the buyer $100 and donated it to the Colorado Historical Society.

A second auction at the house in 1989 consisted largely of post-Hill items, most of them from the Town Club, which purchased the mansion from the Hill estate in 1955. Today, the grand house that was the scene of so many gay gatherings houses the offices of the law firm of Haddon, Morgan and Foreman.

It was left to brilliant and erudite *Rocky Mountain News* columnist Lee Casey to sum up Louise Hill's place in local society following the 1947 auction: "I prefer to think the laughter at the Crawford Hill auction was evidence of nervousness and not of mirth. For there is nothing funny in the end of an era. The Sacred 36 ... were men and women of polish, people who knew how to eat properly and talk properly, two arts that are threatening to become wholly lost."

SOURCES

Books

Bartlett, Ichabod. *History of Wyoming*. Chicago: S. J. Clarke, 1918.

Blair, Charles, with John Sherrill and Elizabeth Sherrill. *The Man Who Could Do No Wrong*. Lincoln, VA: Chosen Books, 1981.

Blum, Deborah. *The Poisoner's Handbook: Murder and the Birth of Forensic Medicine in Jazz Age New York*. New York: Penguin, 2010.

Butler, Anne M. *Daughters of Joy, Sisters of Misery: Prostitutes in the American West, 1865–90*. Urbana: University of Illinois Press, 1985.

Casey, Lee, ed. *Denver Murders*. New York: Duell, Sloan and Pearce, 1946.

Faulkner, Debra B. *Ladies of the Brown: A Women's History of Denver's Most Elegant Hotel*. Charleston, SC: The History Press, 2010.

Fetter, Richard L., and Suzanne C. Fetter. *Telluride: From Pick to Powder*. Caldwell, ID: Caxton Press, 1979.

Fowler, Gene. *Timber Line*. New York: Garden City Books, 1951.

Goodstein, Phil. *Denver from the Bottom Up: A People's History of Early Colorado*. Denver: New Social Publications, 2003.

———. *The Ghosts of Denver: Capitol Hill*. Denver: New Social Publications, 1996.

Hosokawa, Bill. *Thunder in the Rockies: The Incredible Denver Post*. New York: Morrow, 1976.

Iversen, Kristen. *Molly Brown: Unraveling the Myth*. Boulder, CO: Johnson Books, 1999.

Jividen, Doris. *Sammy Amalu: Prince, Pauper or Phony?* Honolulu: Erin Enterprises, 1972.

Johnson, Charles A. *Denver's Mayor Speer*. Denver: Green Mountain Press, 1969.

Kreck, Dick. *Murder at the Brown Palace: A True Story of Seduction and Betrayal*. Golden, CO: Fulcrum Publishing, 2003.

Lukas, J. Anthony. *Big Trouble: A Murder in a Small Western Town Sets Off a Struggle for the Soul of America*. New York: Simon & Schuster, 1997.

McCartney, Laton. *The Teapot Dome Scandal*. New York: Random House, 2008.

Perkin, Robert. *The First Hundred Years: An Informal History of Denver and the Rocky Mountain News*. New York: Doubleday, 1959.

Queen, Ellery. *The Woman in the Case*. New York: Bantam, 1966.

Riley, Marilyn Griggs. *High Altitude Attitudes: Six Savvy Colorado Women*. Boulder, CO: Johnson Books, 2006.

Robinson, David. *Chaplin: His Life and Art*. New York: McGraw-Hill, 1985.

Secrest, Clark. *Hell's Belles: Denver's Brides of the Multitudes, with Attention to Various Gamblers, Scoundrels, and Mountebanks and a Short Biography of Sam Howe, Frontier Lawman*. Denver: Hindsight Historical Publications, 1996.

Smiley, Jerome C. *History of Denver with Outlines of the Earlier History of the Rocky Mountain Country*. Denver: Times-Sun Publishing Co., 1901.

Smith, H. Allen. *To Hell in a Handbasket: The Education of a Humorist*. New York: Doubleday, 1962.

Student, Annette L. *Denver's Riverside Cemetery: Where History Lies*. San Diego, CA: CSN Books, 2006.

Wallace, Elizabeth Victoria. *Hidden History of Denver*. Charleston, SC: The History Press, 2011.

Washburn, Josie. *The Underworld Sewer: A Prostitute Reflects on Life in the Trade, 1871–1909*. Urbana-Champaign: University of Illinois, 1909 (1987 reprint).

Articles

Bliven, Bruce. "Tempest Over a Teapot." *American Heritage 16*, no. 2 (August 1965)

Cour, Robert. "What Is Pearl O'Loughlin's Secret?" *Empire Magazine, The Denver Post*, April 8, 1951.

Fenwick, Robert W. "Can Fred Ward Make a Million?" *Empire Magazine, The Denver Post*, April 11, 1954.

Gibbard, Frank. "Brutality and Redemption: The Pearl O'Loughlin Case." *The Colorado Lawyer 40*, no. 6 (June 2011).

Griggs, Marilyn. "Louise Sneed Hill: She Scandalized Denver's Old Guard." *Colorado Homes & Lifestyles*, March/April 1986.

Kalette, Denise. "A Pastor and His Flock." *Aurora Sentinel*, June 22, 1977.

Keating, Barbara J. "Denver's Mrs. Crawford Hill." *Historic Denver News*, June 1983.

Lipsey, John Johnson. "Alias Diamond Jack." *Denver Posse Brand Book*, 1955.

Prendergast, Alan. "The Promise That Died with Pastor Charles Blair." *Westword*, August 24, 2009.

Ward, Iva, as told to Bernice Morgan. "My Life with Fred Ward," *Empire Magazine, The Denver Post*, October 14, 1951.

Additional Resources for Historical Research

Castle Rock, Colorado, Historical Society and Museum.

Federal Bureau of Investigation Organized-Crime Memos. Unnamed agent to FBI director, July 23, 1935, and Special Agent D. M. Ladd to FBI director, March 19, 1937. Douglas County History Research Center, Castle Rock, Colorado.

Letter from H. H. Tammen to George B. Christian Jr., secretary to President Warren Harding, *The Denver Post*, August 5, 1922.

Letter from Mrs. Crawford Hill to American League to Abolish Capital Punishment, May 14, 1931, Sneed Hill Collection MSS309 FF 53, Stephen H. Hart Library and Research Center, History Colorado.

Royal Gorge Regional Museum & History Center, Cañon City, Colorado.

Newspapers
Chicago Examiner
The Denver Daily Times

The Denver Post
The Denver Republican
The Denver Times
Denver Tribune
The Gazette, Colorado Springs
Golden (Colorado) Daily Transcript
Golden (Colorado) Weekly Globe
Idaho Statesman, Boise
Kansas City (Missouri) Star
Los Angeles Examiner
The New York Globe
The New York Times
Omaha World-Herald
The Oregonian, Portland
Pueblo Chieftain
Riverside (California) Daily Press
Rocky Mountain Herald, Denver
Rocky Mountain News, Denver
The San Francisco Call
The San Francisco Examiner
Springfield (Illinois) Union

About the Author

Dick Kreck retired from *The Denver Post* after 38 years as an editor and columnist. He previously worked at the *San Francisco Examiner* and the *Los Angeles Times*. He is the author of six other books, including *Murder at the Brown Palace: A True Story of Seduction and Betrayal* and *Smaldone: The Untold Story of an American Crime Family*. He lives in Denver, Colorado.